The Clean Water Act:

THE SECOND DECADE

Morris A. Ward

E. BRUCE HARRISON COMPANY
Washington, D.C.

ISBN 0-9609130-0-9
Library of Congress Catalog Card Number 82-82260

The Clean Water Act: The Second Decade
published by
The E. Bruce Harrison Company
605 14th Street, NW
Washington, DC 20005

PREFACE

The Nation's effort to collectively address water pollution problems is now ten years old. Ten years is not a very long time for a social, economic and engineering effort on the scale called for in the Federal Water Pollution Control Act of 1972—to clean the Nation's waterways and keep them clean. Like other national environmental control efforts, "clean water" activities are substantially more recent than most of the other social movements which have characterized the United States as it moves into its third century.

Which is not to say that there had not already been some states and some industries moving ahead with water pollution control efforts in 1972, when Congress passed the third major component of what then-President Richard M. Nixon declared "the environmental decade." Much engineering thinking and some actual installation and operation of pollution control "hardware" was under way when the amendments took their place beside the National Environmental Policy Act (NEPA) and the Clean Air Act (both passed two years earlier) as the foundation of U.S. pollution-control policy.

While the implementation of the Clean Water Act has not always been smooth — and while few would question that some water quality gains might have been achieved more economically or more efficiently — few observers doubt that the Nation's Clean Water Act has protected water quality and prevented further degradation. If only by holding water pollution concentrations steady in the face of growing population and an expanding industrial base, the Clean Water Act has proven beneficial.

But it is not necessarily perfect. After ten years, almost any program needs reconditioning and review — particularly a program of the enormous complexity and comprehensiveness of the clean water campaign.

Fortunately, Congress did not expect the clean water engine to run indefinitely without a fine-tuning. It provided that the Clean Water Act be subject to extension —reauthorization—in 1982.

It is that process of review which this publication is intended to serve. By providing an overview of the entire Act and a section-by-section description of its major components, in layman's terms, the book is designed to serve as a source document for all the diverse interests wanting to be involved in the reauthorization of the Clean Water Act. And by providing a descriptive rundown of particular "issues" likely to arise during Congressional deliberations, it should serve as an informative reference for all the disciplines, from the engineering and legal communities to the government relations and public affairs practitioners, whose active involvement is essential to effective public policy-making.

The Clean Water Act itself is recognized as one of the most complex federal legislative and regulatory programs ever adopted, no less complex than the very problems it is meant to address. This book will help all those interested in water quality to cut through some of that complexity and play an active, informed and responsible part in the review and extension of the Act.

About the Author

Morris A. (Bud) Ward for five years was Managing Editor of the Bureau of National Affairs' (BNA) *Environment Reporter.* From March 1979 to May 1981 he was Assistant Director of the National Commission on Air Quality. He prepared this report while working as a private environmental consultant in Washington, D.C. In January 1982, he became Editor of a new monthly magazine, *The Environmental Forum,* which began publication in May 1982 under the auspices of the Environmental Law Institute in Washington, D.C.

Publisher

E. Bruce Harrison Company is a communications management firm specializing in issues communications. The company has been intensively involved in environmental issues, as a consultant to industry and government, since 1973. Numerous articles, newsletters, and pamphlets have been prepared on environmental, energy, and other subjects. THE CLEAN WATER ACT: THE SECOND DECADE is the firm's first published book.

TABLE OF CONTENTS

The Clean Water Act:
The Second Decade

INTRODUCTION

The Nation's efforts to control water pollution date from the enactment in 1972 of the Federal Water Pollution Control Act (Public Law 92-500).

Although that law established the backbone of modern water pollution control initiatives in the United States, it was not the first entry by the federal government into water pollution control activities. The first Federal Water Pollution Control Act, in 1948, was amended five times prior to passage of the 1972 amendments; and several tenets of the 1948 law are embodied in the current law—such as encouragement of interstate compacts (Sec. 103 of current law) and the assignment to states of the primary responsibility for preventing, reducing and eliminating water pollution (Sec. 101(b)).

The 1948 Act espoused a 'water-quality-standards'-approach to water pollution control, meaning that pollution would be regulated by determining the use to which a body of water would be put—fishing, swimming, drinking, industrial uses—with the water quality standard expressing how much pollution can be put into a particular body of water. While identifying the health of the public as being of "paramount importance," the law allowed courts to require reductions in water pollution only after "giving due consideration to the practicability and to the physical and economic feasibility of securing abatement of any pollution proved."[1]

In 1965, Congress adopted amendments providing that water quality standards be established for interstate waters. These standards were to be adopted by states or, lacking state action, by the Secretary of the Interior. They were intended to protect public health or welfare, enhance water quality and otherwise serve the Act's purposes. In setting the standards, the state or Interior Secretary was to consider their value to public water supplies, propagation of fish and wildlife, recreational purposes, and agricultural, industrial and other appropriate uses.[2]

Another forerunner to modern water pollution control legislation in the U.S. was the Rivers and Harbors Appropriations Act of 1899, commonly referred to as the Refuse Act. Unlike the 1948 Act with its dependence on water quality standards, the 1899 law relied on the 'effluent limitations' approach, meaning that effluent standards proscribed the amount of water pollution which could be legally discharged from an individual source, without regard to the water quality of the receiving water body.

Despite enactment of the 1948 and 1965 amendments to the Federal Water Pollution Control Act, until the early 1970s it was largely several states' technology-based standards and the 1899 Rivers and Harbors Act or Refuse Act which served as the basis of water pollution control. That law sought to ban discharges from ships or on-shore facilities of "any refuse matter of any kind or description whatever other than that flowing from streets and sewers and passing therefrom in a liquid state."[3] It sought also to prohibit depositing of materials on banks of navigable waters if those materials could be washed into the water and could impede or obstruct navigation, and violations could be enjoined and

1

punished as criminal actions. The Secretary of the Army, which administered the law through the Corps of Engineers, was authorized to permit discharges as conditioned by him.

Following congressional hearings in 1970 suggesting that thousands of industrial water pollution sources were discharging into navigable waters without permits under the 1899 Act, the Corps of Engineers announced it would adopt new permitting procedures applicable to those industrial dischargers. But on December 23, 1970, then-President Richard M. Nixon pre-empted the Corps by issuing Executive Order 11574 directing adoption of a permitting program under the Rivers and Harbors Act.

At the same time, there was a growing consensus that the water quality standards approach to water pollution control presented difficult or impossible challenges to enforcement and that the approach did not adequately address some water pollutants. In addition, it was increasingly apparent that water quality modeling techniques were not sufficiently sophisticated to determine which individual source's pollution had contributed to the degradation of a water body.

The philosophies behind both the water quality standards approach and the effluent standards approach are well-characterized in the succeeding two paragraphs from William H. Rodgers's *Environmental Law.* The general thinking outlined here by Rodgers was prevalent in Congress and elsewhere in the U.S. in the early 1970s, as the nation was preparing to embark on a new and more ambitious water pollution control effort:

> The water quality standards view of water pollution has many implications. It assumes a free use of water for waste disposal up to a point of "unreasonableness," however legally defined, and that the enforcement authority has the burden of proving that discharges harm marine resources or deter other water uses. It assumes the government should share heavily in research and development costs for controls deviating from the norm of no control. It insists that enforcement is a particularly local concern because the unique characteristics of the receiving water, the economies of the discharging plant, and even the prevailing political tolerance level are relevant to decisions to compel treatment or process change. Early versions of the Federal Water Pollution Control Act adhered closely to these premises.
>
> The "no discharge" prohibitions of the Rivers and Harbors Act look the other way. They focus on the source—not the size, flow and uses of the receiving body of water. Pollution dilution is not part of the lexicon. The concept is absolutist. Rationalization about "reasonable" amounts of pollution is not easily reconciled with a statute declaring it a crime to dump "refuse of any kind or description whatever" into navigable waters. While water quality standards appeal to economic and biological reality, effluent standards are more attuned to political necessity.[4]

Congressional debate leading up to enactment of the Federal Water Pollution Control Act Amendments of 1972 in the largest sense involved differences over the water quality standards and effluent standards approaches. As is often the case in the political arena, given such basic philosophical differences, neither side won unequivocally. As a result, the 1972 Act contains elements of both strategies — although few question that it was clearly the effluent standards approach which assumed a dominant role, with water quality standards now serving what Rodgers calls "an important interstitial function."[5]

The 1972 Water Act Amendments

The 1972 amendments to the Federal Water Pollution Control Act represent not just amendments to an existing law but, in effect, an entirely new law—a "massive new effort"[6] calling for reduction and even elimination of the flow of water pollution from both municipal sewage systems and industrial facilities. Based largely on an effluent standards approach, the new law abandoned reliance on professional judgments about a particular water body's "assimilative capacity." It established strategies intended to achieve the national goal (not requirement, but goal) of zero-discharge of water pollution by 1985. As an interim requirement, the law set a July 1, 1983, deadline by which time the nation's waters were to be "fishable and swimmable."

The amendments authorized billions of dollars of federal assistance for construction of municipal wastewater treatment facilities. In addition, Section 208 required development of comprehensive areawide waste treatment management plans covering both "point sources" (those emitting from a specific, discernible conduit or discharge pipe) and "nonpoint sources" (for which pollutants are not associated with a discrete conveyance but rather flow generally — agricultural fields, construction sites, urban streets, mining and timbering activities, etc.)

Additional highlights of the Federal Water Pollution Control Act Amendments of 1972 include the following provisions:

- The Act established three phases of nationally uniform effluent limitations for industrial dischargers:
  — industrial dischargers were to achieve best practicable technology (BPT) by July 1, 1977;
  — industrial dischargers were to achieve a more stringent best available technology (BAT) by July 1, 1983; and
  — upon commencing operation, new industrial sources were to achieve new source performance standards.
- Section 307 established special controls for toxic water pollutants.
- Section 402 established the National Pollutant Discharge Elimination System (NPDES), providing for issuance, renewal and upgrading of permits for all point sources of water pollution. This established the first major direct enforcement procedure against sources discharging water pollution without an adequate permit.
- Section 404 established a program applying specifically to the handling of dredged or fill materials, to be administered by the Corps of Engineers.
- The Act required national effluent limitations for publicly-owned wastewater treatment works, providing federal funding for planning and construction and establishing best practicable technology and best available technology deadlines.

The 1977 Water Act Amendments

In 1977 Congress changed the name of the Federal Water Pollution Control Act to the Clean Water Act. This change reflected an increased sensitivity to the negative connotations associated in certain segments of society with the words "federal" and "control" — and certainly capitalized on the political difficulties of voting against a bill so benignly titled.* Who could vote against clean water, after all?

Although its name changed, the overall thrust of the law did not, as Congress retained its commitment to an effluent standards-based statute. Nonetheless, Congress made some significant changes, most significantly by redirecting the emphasis of the program to the control of toxic water pollutants.

For industrial dischargers, the 1977 Act specifies three sets of effluent limitations to be met by deadlines ranging from July 1, 1983, to July 1, 1987:

- Best conventional technology (BCT), roughly equivalent to secondary treatment requirements for municipal dischargers, had to be achieved by July 1, 1984 for sources discharging the kinds of conventional pollutants generally found in domestic discharges.

- Best available technology economically achievable (BAT) had to be achieved by July 1, 1984, for dischargers of priority toxic pollutants specified in a consent decree reached by the Natural Resources Defense Council (NRDC) and the Environmental Protection Agency.

- BAT for dischargers of nonconventional pollutants (neither conventional nor specified in the law as presumed to be toxic) was to be achieved no later than July 1, 1987.

For municipal facilities, Congress extended the best practical technology deadline for five years to 1983. Congress also authorized that states could be delegated management of the construction grants program for publicly-owned treatment works. The 1977 Act reflected increased Congressional interest in stimulating nontraditional, innovative, cost-effective and environmentally-sound systems of treating wastes. It included incentives to promote recycling and reuse of pollution control byproducts such as effluent, sludge and nutrients and to increase energy conservation. In addition, the 1977 Act held out the prospect for multi-year reauthorization of the sewage treatment plant construction grants program, with a total authorization of $25.5 billion through September 30, 1982.

The 1981 Water Act Amendments

Congress in 1981 passed, and the President signed into law, the "Municipal Wastewater Treatment Construction Grant Amendments of 1981." The amendments provide funding authorizations of $2.4 billion per fiscal year for the fiscal years ending on September 30 of 1982, 1983, 1984, and 1985. They also address substantive issues involving eligibility for federal grant awards, reserve capacity for funding projected future growth, and the appropriate federal share for funding of treatment works.

---

*The Senate and House in fact disagreed on the name of the Act, and they compromised by using both the new and old titles, calling it "The Federal Water Pollution Control Act (commonly called the Clean Water Act)."

4

OVERVIEW OF THE CLEAN WATER ACT

The Clean Water Act is intended to provide a comprehensive programmatic and regulatory approach to water pollution control. Like the natural ecosystem it is designed to protect, the Act itself consists of many closely inter-related components which should be viewed not as separate and discrete entities but rather as parts of a single package.

The Act consists of five titles. Title I specifies the overall goal of the Clean Water Act—"to restore and maintain the chemical, physical, and biological integrity of the Nation's waters." It establishes as a national goal the elimination of discharges of pollutants into the nation's navigable waters by 1985. Where attainable, it sets a July 1, 1983, goal that water quality provide for the protection and propagation of fish, shellfish and wildlife.

Section 101 establishes as national policy the prohibition of discharges of toxic water pollutants in toxic amounts. It provides federal funds for construction of publicly-owned wastewater treatment works, and calls for a major research and development effort to eliminate water pollution discharges. Title I also details research and development activities, establishes funding for those activities and calls for interstate cooperation.

Title II of the Act establishes procedures for federal financial assistance for publicly-owned treatment works. It specifies the federal share of that funding, and details procedures for priority determinations and cost-effectiveness guidelines. Section 208 establishes an extensive program by which states are to develop and put into effect areawide waste treatment management plans.

Title III of the Act establishes a series of progressively more stringent effluent limitations, and calls for state adoption and federal approval of water quality-related standards for interstate waters. It also provides for toxic water pollutant effluent standards and for pretreatment of industrial wastewaters prior to their being discharged to a publicly-owned treatment works. Title III calls for enforcement, inspection and monitoring activities to assure compliance with the Act's provisions. In addition, it establishes control programs specifically aimed at oil and hazardous substances, thermal discharges, pollution from marine sanitation devices, and abatement of international water pollution.

Title IV of the Clean Water Act establishes the National Pollutant Discharge Elimination System (NPDES), through which discharges of water pollutants into navigable waters must receive permits from the appropriate federal, state or interstate agency. Discharges without applicable permits are unlawful. Title IV also calls for establishment of criteria applicable to discharges to the ocean, creates a permitting program administered by the Corps of Engineers for dredged or fill materials, and provides for disposal of sewage sludges.

Title V contains provisions involving administration, general definitions, and

5

establishment of a water pollution control advisory board to assist the Environmental Protection Agency in carrying out the Act. It provides for judicial review and reports to Congress.

Taken collectively, implementation of the five individual titles is intended to lead to attainment of the Act's overall requirement of assuring that the nation's waters are "fishable and swimmable." Step-by-step application of the five titles' separate components theoretically leads to the national goal of eliminating discharges of pollution to the nation's waterways. With municipal dischargers permitted under Section 402 and regulated largely under Title II, and industrial dischargers permitted under Section 402 of Title IV; with increasingly stringent effluent limitations specified for both municipal and industrial effluents under Title III; with special water pollution problems addressed under Titles III and IV; with administration and enforcement spelled out in Titles III, IV, and V; and with nonpoint sources of water pollution addressed under Title II, the Clean Water Act is intended to correct existing water pollution problems and maintain water quality where it exists.

With that broad overview, succeeding sections of this report will describe the individual provisions of the Clean Water Act in further detail. These sections will specify how those provisions are intended to work in conjunction with other aspects, and explore issues which have arisen as the Act has been implemented.

TITLE I
RESEARCH AND RELATED PROGRAMS

Section-By-Section Analysis

Section 101

In declaring the goals and policy of the Clean Water Act in Section 101, Congress established that the objective of the law is to "restore and maintain the chemical, physical, and biological integrity of the Nation's waters."[7]

To achieve that general but ambitious objective, Congress established several goals and national policies: elimination of discharges of water pollutants by 1985; fishable/swimmable waters by July 1, 1983; prohibition on discharge of "toxic pollutants in toxic amounts;" availability of federal funding for construction of publicly-owned treatment works; development and implementation of areawide waste treatment planning processes; and encouragement of research and demonstration projects to assure that technology will be available to eliminate water pollution discharges.

In addition to encouraging international cooperation on water pollution control matters, Section 101 directs the Environmental Protection Agency (EPA), the agency administering the law, to provide for, encourage, and assist in development of effective public participation in carrying out standards, regulations, effluent limitations and plans under the Act. It establishes as national policy a "drastic minimization of paperwork and interagency decision procedures," as well as the prevention of "needless duplication and unnecessary delays at all levels of government."

Finally, Section 101 was amended in 1977 to make clear that Congress did not intend the Act to lead to a reduction in the quantities of water allocated to particular states. Congress directed federal agencies, in carrying out the programs under the Act, to make sure that they seek to control water pollution in ways consistent with managing overall water resources. This amendment was intended not to change existing law but rather to clarify Congressional intent.

In Section 101(b), Congress restated its intention to recognize and preserve "the primary responsibilities and rights" of states to prevent, reduce and eliminate water pollution. Not satisfied with the extent to which such state delegation was proceeding, Congress in the 1977 Amendments specifically added that it wanted states to manage the sewage treatment plan construction grants program and the Section 402 (NPDES) and 404 (dredged or fill materials) permitting programs.

Sections 102, 103, 104, 105

Section 102 of the Clean Water Act is a continuation of the authority for EPA to conduct comprehensive water quality management planning.

⌈ Section 103 continues provisions of earlier laws encouraging the Federal Government to promote and encourage efforts among states to work together to control water pollution. It approves agreements or compacts among two or more states for prevention and control of pollution and for enforcement of their respective water pollution control laws. But it also specifies that those agreements are not binding unless and until approved by Congress.⌋

Section 104 expands the responsibilities and authorities of the EPA Administrator in water pollution control research. It authorizes establishment of field research laboratories throughout the country, directs a study of Great Lakes water quality and of public health and public welfare effects of water pollution, and directs a study of practices for disposing of used engine, machine and cooling oils. Congress amended Section 104 in 1977 to direct the EPA Administrator to establish (or contract with an appropriate nonprofit organization for establishment of) a national clearinghouse to receive Water Act research reports and provide for them to be distributed.

Section 105-115

The remainder of Title I involves research, development and demonstration projects and special studies to be conducted on water pollution control. It specifies federal funding restrictions for research and development activities, as well as for grants to state and interstate agencies to carry out pollution control activities. Section 107 directs a study of mining acidity and other water pollution problems. Section 108 covers demonstration projects involving pollution control in all or any part of the watersheds of the Great Lakes. Section 109 deals with training grants and contracts with educational institutions to produce properly-trained personnel for carrying out requirements of the Act.

Sections 110 and 111 of the Act involve training grants and contracts and awards of scholarships for future sewage treatment plant operators. Section 112 specifies definitions for terms used in Sections 109 through 112 (e.g., "institution of higher learning", "academic year").

Sections 113 and 114 respectively call for a demonstration project on safe water and elimination or control of water pollution for native villages in Alaska and a study of the "fragile ecology" of Lake Tahoe. Section 115 calls for a study to identify in-place toxic pollutants in harbors and navigable waterways, authorizes the EPA Administrator to contract through the Secretary of the Army for the removal and appropriate disposal of such toxic materials from "critical" port and harbor areas, and authorizes $15,000,000 for these activities.

Legislative Issues

Although Section 101 is not a substantive or regulatory component of the overall statute, aspects of the section do provoke criticisms in certain quarters. It is likely that a comprehensive review of the Clean Water Act would lead to suggestions that Congress re-evaluate those parts of Section 101.

Critics have pointed out, for instance, that the "restore and maintain" language —comparable in some ways to the "protect and enhance" terminology in the goals section of the Clean Air Act—is indefinite: Restore to what point? To the level of water quality that existed twenty years ago? Thirty years ago? Forty? Fifty? Or, since the term appears unqualified, is water quality to be "restored" to its status as of the start of the Industrial Revolution? Or as of the beginning of recorded history?

In the end, however, this debate may be left to the philosophers and academicians; to legislators, the language is routinely accepted as a not-uncommon rhetorical flourish. More likely to be challenged is retention in the Act of the stated national goal of *eliminating* all water pollution discharges by 1985.

Critics of that goal (again, it is important to emphasize that the zero-discharge provision, leading in theory to dry discharge pipes, is a goal and not a requirement) argue with abundant justification that achieving it would be prohibitively expensive. Perhaps equally important, critics of the zero-discharge goal say it would reduce by one-third the available media into which wastes can be disposed—air, land and water. Movement toward such a goal might compromise the integrity of air and land resources without regard for which of the three environmental media is best suited to accommodate a given quantity or type of waste product. Even if zero discharge were economically attractive, would it be environmentally desirable?

While acknowledging the validity of such concerns, defenders of the zero-discharge goal are quick to point out that it *is* a goal and not a requirement. They also point out that in certain industrial applications zero-discharge is not only environmentally acceptable but also financially beneficial to the source. Given its technology-forcing implications and assuming it continues to be administered not as a proscription but as a goal, they say, why eliminate it?

Given the symbolic importance of the zero-discharge goal in some quarters and the reaction in others that nonsensical goals should not be tolerated even if they are "just" goals, it is possible that Congress would consider a compromise. One concept (embodied in the 1972 House bill but dropped by the 1972 House/Senate conference) would have required agencies carrying out the law to consider potential impacts of their activities on water, land and air resources. As the House Public Works and Transportation Committee said at the time, "There is little to be gained in stopping water pollution if the preventive actions cause more environmental damage than they eliminate."[8]

TITLE II

GRANTS FOR CONSTRUCTION OF TREATMENT WORKS

Title II of the Clean Water Act contains major provisions for water quality management planning and for funding and construction of publicly-owned wastewater treatment works.

In the 1972 Amendments to Title II, Congress established one of the largest and most ambitious domestic public works projects in the Nation's history, with an initial three-year authorization of $18 billion in 75-percent federal grants to municipalities for construction of sewage treatment plants and systems. The 1972 Amendments specified that municipalities provide at least the equivalent of secondary treatment for municipal wastes — meaning that 85 percent of the conventional pollutants in municipal wastes were to be removed by no later than July 1, 1977. Municipalities were to achieve "best practicable" wastewater treatment technology, a stringent control requiring removal of additional pollution, by July 1, 1983.

In the 1977 Clean Water Act Amendments, Congress extended to 1983 the deadline for municipalities to meet the secondary treatment requirement. It also increased to $44 billion the total federal money available for municipal construction grants.

Congress again amended the Act four years later, by passing the "Municipal Wastewater Treatment Construction Grant Amendments of 1981." Signed by President Reagan late in 1981, the law provides a $2.4 billion authorization for the construction grants program for fiscal 1982. It also addresses funding eligibility and procedural aspects of the grants program, and its enactment makes further consideration of substantive Clean Water Act Title II issues unlikely in the 1982 debate on amendments.

Section-By-Section Analysis

Section 201 (Purpose)

Section 201 establishes as the goal of Title II the development and implementation of waste treatment management plans and practices which will lead to achievement of the Act's overall goals through application of best practicable waste treatment technology. Waste treatment should be conducted on an areawide basis where possible and should provide for control or treatment of both point sources and nonpoint sources of pollution. The EPA Administrator is directed to encourage facilities providing for recycling of sewage pollutants, confined and contained disposal of pollutants not recycled, wastewater reclamation, and non-polluting disposal of sewage sludges.

Section 201 precludes federal grants to state or municipal agencies, or any combination of such agencies, if they have not evaluated potential uses of alternative waste management techniques. As part of the 1977 amendments, Congress mandated that grant applicants demonstrate that they have fully studied innovative and alternative wastewater treatment processes as well as techniques providing for wastewater reclamation and reuse. It also directed EPA to encourage energy-saving waste treatment measures.

As part of the 1981 amendments, Congress narrowed the number of categories eligible for federal funding. It said that grants made after October 1, 1984, can be made only for projects of secondary or more stringent standards, for new interceptor sewers and their appurtenances, and for correction of infiltration-in-flow problems. As of enactment of the 1981 amendments, grants no longer could be made for funding just facility plans or for funding plans, specifications and estimates for a proposed project. In addition, Congress made special allowance for grants as of October 1, 1984, to address combined storm water and sanitary sewer overflows not otherwise eligible for federal funding. It also designated that $200 million be available each fiscal year for addressing water quality problems of marine bays and estuaries affected by combined sewer overflow problems.

Section 202 (Federal Share)

Section 202 established a 75-percent federal funding share for construction of treatment works. In the 1977 Amendments Congress specified that grants made between September 30, 1978, and October 1, 1981, would be 85 percent of the construction costs if the grantee used innovative or alternative wastewater treatment processes as discussed under Section 201.

In the 1981 amendments Congress directed that the 75 percent federal funding share which has characterized the water quality program since 1972 come to an end in 1984. Beginning in October 1984, the federal government will pay 55 percent of the construction costs for eligible projects.

Section 203 (Plans, Specifications, Estimates and Payments)

Using as a model the Federal Aid Highway Act, Congress in Section 203 directed that grant applicants provide plans, specifications and estimates (PS&E) for each proposed project for which federal funds are requested. Under the three-step grants process, an applicant files PS&E for a project to determine the feasibility of a treatment works and a second set of PS&E for engineering, architectural, legal, fiscal or economic reviews. A third set of PS&E is prepared for actual construction of the treatment works. EPA approval of a set of plans, specifications and estimates obligates the U.S. Government to pay 75 percent of that step of the project.

In the 1977 Amendments to the Clean Water Act, Congress moved to streamline the three-step grants process as it applies to smaller treatment works. Specifically, Congress amended Section 203(a) to authorize the EPA Administrator to issue a combined Step II/III grant covering the federal share for both preparation of construction plans and specifications, and for building of the treatment works. These combined grants are limited to treatment works for which the EPA Administrator estimates a total cost of $2 million or less ($3 million in states with "unusually high costs of construction," such as Alaska). Another limitation on the combined grants is that the municipality applying have a population of no more than 25,000 people according to the most recent U.S. census.

Section 204 (Limitations and Conditions)

Section 204 details conditions which must be met by grant applicants prior to EPA approval of federal funding. For instance, treatment works for which funding is applied must be included in applicable Section 208 areawide waste treatment management plans (described below). They must also conform with state water quality standards adopted under Section 303(e) of the Act (also described below). Grant applicants agree to pay non-federal costs and to assure proper and efficient operation of the treatment works, including employment of trained management and operations personnel.

Section 204(a)(5) requires that the size and capacity of the treatment works be directly related to the needs it is intended to serve, "including sufficient reserve capacity." The "reserve capacity" provision authorizes EPA and states to plan for and fund future growth in population and pollution sources. Critics of the program accuse some plants of being "gold-plated," and say that this provision encourages uncontrolled and unplanned growth characterized as "urban sprawl."

It was in response to that criticism that Congress in the 1981 amendments limited federal funding for reserve capacity as of October 1, 1984. The new law says grants made after that date may be made only for needs existing on the date of the step three grant, and in no case for needs existing only after September 30, 1990.

A major part of Section 204 is the provision in Section 204(b) requiring that grant applicants adopt a system of user charges designed to assure that sources discharging to publicly-owned treatment works pay their "proportionate share" of operation and maintenance costs. In the March 1972 House Committee on Public Works report on the Federal Water Pollution Control Act Amendments of 1972, the rationale behind the user charges concept was explained in the following way:

> The Committee believes it is essential to the successful operation by public agencies that a system of fair and equitable user charges be established....This section contains standards the Committee believes should be taken into account by the Administrator; foremost among these is the underlying objective of achieving a local system that is self-sufficient.

> In connection with industrial users of publicly-owned systems, the Committee desired to establish within the user charge system an arrangement whereby industrial users would pay charges sufficient to bear their fair portion of all costs including the share of federal contributions for capital construction attributable to that part of the cost of constructed facilities attributable to use by industrial sources. It is the Committee's view that it is inappropriate in a large federal grant program providing a high percentage of construction funds to subsidize industrial users from funds provided by the taxpayers at large.[9]

Section 204 was subject to substantial amendment in 1977, particularly those provisions dealing with reserve capacity, user charges and industrial cost recovery. On the reserve capacity issue, Congress amended Section 204(a)(5) to require the EPA administrator to take into account efforts to reduce total sewage flow and unnecessary water consumption. It limited grant-eligibility to that reserve capacity needed to serve projected population and associated commercial and industrial growth identified in treatment works facilities plans or in Section 208 areawide plans.

The 1977 amendments provide for use of *ad valorem* taxes as a basis for assessing user charges. This provision avoids the prohibitively expensive and administratively difficult approach of metering all sewage flows as a basis for establishing contributions to treatment plant financing.

The 1977 Senate bill to amend the Federal Water Pollution Control Act (S. 1952) would have allowed exemptions from industrial cost recovery provisions for industrial sources discharging less than 2,500 gallons a day to a treatment works. This exemption recognized the administrative difficulties facing municipalities in attempting to design equitable cost recovery programs. As finally adopted in the 1977 Amendments, the provision exempts from industrial cost recovery requirements industrial sources discharging less than 250,000 gallons a day so long as they do not introduce pollutants interfering with, contaminating or reducing the use of the treatment work's sludge.

Despite that effort to acknowledge the administrative problems, Congress decided that more was needed. It authorized an 18-month moratorium on federal enforcement of the program, saying EPA should continue to make grants during that time nothwithstanding the absence of a cost recovery program.

In the 1981 amendments, Congress terminated the industrial cost exclusion program as of November 15, 1981.

Section 205 (Allotment)

Section 205 details the politically sensitive formula by which legislators agree on what percentage of the federal funding is to be made available to individual states. The 1972 Amendments replaced the original formula based on population with one intended to reflect actual waste treatment needs of individual states.

Section 206 (Reimbursement and Advanced Construction)

Section 206 provides for federal reimbursements to municipalities for treatment works constructed without federal contributions. Since the agencies' commitments of their own funds to prefinance a portion of the federal share had facilitated water pollution cleanup, Congress decided that reimbursements were a matter of equity.

Section 207 (Authorizations)

Section 207 authorizes maximum appropriations to be made available by Congress for funding the federal share of the sewage treatment plant construction grants program. After authorizing an initial three-year appropriation of $18 billion as part of the 1972 Amendments, in 1977 Congress authorized a funding ceiling of $24.5 billion over five fiscal years— $4.5 billion in fiscal 1978 and $5 billion each year in fiscal 1979, 1980, 1981, and 1982.

Despite those lofty funding authorizations, actual appropriations for construction of sewage treatment projects have been far less than Congress has authorized.

States have criticized the substantial uncertainty associated with the program; of the $18 billion initially authorized by Congress over three years, for instance, $9 million was impounded by then-President Nixon until the Supreme Court eventually overturned the impoundment.

One major 1977 amendment was adopted in order to comply with the Congressional Budget and Impoundment Control Act. The amendment—making each authorization specifically subject to subsequent appropriation acts—was recognized as reintroducing "the very uncertainty in the level of federal funding" that Congress had wanted to eliminate.[10] The House and Senate conferees said they "hope and expect" that the House and Senate appropriations committees would provide advanced appropriations for fiscal years 1979, 1980 and 1981. "Only in this way," they said, "can states and communities know in advance that adequate funds will be available and proceed to plan for construction of needed wastewater treatment works."[11]

The 1981 Act authorizes $2.4 billion for each fiscal year from 1982 through September 30, 1985.

Section 208 (Areawide Waste Treatment Management)

Section 208 areawide planning requirements have been characterized by the District Court of the District of Columbia as providing the "critical" elements of a "far-reaching" statute.[12] That assessment does not seem to be overstated, given the Senate and House conferees' 1972 conference agreement:

> The planning process authorized in this section when implemented will provide an identification of the problems, a strategy of solution, implementation of the strategy and evaluation of its effectiveness in accomplishing the desired objectives. The planning process will provide a management concept to coordinate the many separate requirements of this legislation in an effective attack for restoring our Nation's waters.[13]

Section 208 establishes rigid time limits within which governors are to designate, in accordance with EPA regulagulations, areas with "substantial water quality control problems." Governors are then to assign to a single representative organization the responsibilities for devising a comprehensive areawide waste treatment management plan for each area.* Those organizations are to develop plans and submit them to EPA for approval.

Section 208 outlines minimum requirements for the areawide plans:

- They are to identify treatment works needed to meet anticipated municipal and industrial needs over 20 years, with the plans updated annually. These include requirements for acquisition of land for treatment purposes as well as open space and recreation opportunities expected as a result of improved water quality.

- They must set priorities for construction of the treatment works, and time schedules for construction of each treatment works.

---

* The District Court for the District of Columbia (see footnote 11) ruled that states carry out for areas not "designated" as causing "substantial water quality control problems" the same planning as required under Section 208 for areas so designated.

- They must provide for establishment of regulations that: carry out Section 201 waste treatment management requirements; control location, modification and construction of any facility discharging water pollutants in the area; and assure that industrial or commercial wastes discharged into any treatment works in the area meet applicable pretreatment requirements.

- They must identify agencies needed to construct, operate and maintain all facilities required by the plan or otherwise needed to carry out the 208 plan.

- They must identify operational issues such as financial sources, time-frames, total costs, and economic, social, and environmental impacts of carrying out the plan.

- They must include a process for identifying nonpoint sources of water pollution and set forth procedures for controlling those sources, including application of land use requirements.

- They must include a process for controlling disposal of pollutants on land or in underground excavations while protecting groundwater and surface water quality.

The sweeping nature of 208 areawide planning and the theoretical significance of 208 plans to the overall structure of the Clean Water Act are illustrated in the Section 208(e) mandate that National Pollutant Discharge Elimination System (NPDES) permits under Section 402 cannot be issued for any point source which is in conflict with an approved Section 208 plan. Since the Water Act forbids discharges of pollutants into navigable waters from point sources *not* having a valid NPDES permit, Section 208 can appropriately be viewed as the "backbone" of the law.

Congress clearly intended Section 208 planning to relate closely to the construction of treatment works (Section 201) and to the issuance of discharge permits to industrial sources (Section 402). It also directed that 208 plans be consistent with state water quality standards adopted under Section 303(e) and with the dredged or fill materials program under Section 404.

By tying together all of the control programs under the Act—and by therefore bringing together the control of water pollution from all varieties of sources: industrial, municipal and nonpoint — Section 208 is intended to serve as a "control tower." Through it planning, implementation and performance can all be monitored and necessary revisions and adjustments can be identified and put into effect.

Sections 209-218

Section 209 of the Clean Water Act directs the President, through the Water Resources Council, to develop along with state and local interests river basin plans considering both water quantity and water quality issues.

Section 210 requires the EPA Administrator to conduct annual surveys to determine the operating and maintenance efficiency of treatment works constructed with federal funds made available under the Act.

In Section 211, Congress authorizes EPA to award grants for sewage collection systems in existing communities, if the collectors are needed to provide effective and economical operation of a treatment works. This amendment, passed in 1972, came in response to Congressional testimony indicating that construction of waste treatment facilities was frequently delayed because public agencies could not arrange for the financing of collection systems.

Section 212 defines terms as they are used in Title II of the Act.

Section 213 authorizes the EPA Administrator to guarantee the principal and interest on loans or obligations of public agencies in financing non-federal costs of building publicly-owned treatment works.

Section 214, added in the 1977 Amendments, requires the EPA Administrator to develop and operate a continuing public information/public education program on recycling and reuse of wastewater and sludge, use of land treatment, and methods for reducing the volume of wastewater.

Section 215 is a "Buy America" provision encouraging use of domestically-manufactured components in publicly-owned treatment works for which funds are applied under the Act. It allows for exceptions when EPA decides domestically-produced components are too costly or not available, or when multilateral government procurement agreements would be violated.

In 1977 Congress added Section 216 specifying that states and not EPA may determine the funding priority to be assigned to a specific category of projects. Those categories include secondary treatment, treatment more stringent than secondary treatment as needed to meet water quality standards, correction of infiltration/inflow, major sewer system rehabilitation, new collector sewers and appurtenances, new interceptor sewers and appurtenances, and correction of combined sewer overflows. But rather than giving states a completely free hand in determining those funding priorities, Congress said that the EPA Administrator, after a public hearing, could remove a project from a state's priority list if it would not result in compliance with enforceable requirements of the Act.

In Section 217, also added as part of the 1977 Amendments, Congress said that cost-effectiveness guidelines published by EPA must provide for identification and selection of cost-effective alternatives to comply with the objectives and goals of the Act and of Sections 201(b), 201(d), 201(g)(2)(A), and 301(b)(2)(B) of the Act.

A new Section 218, passed in 1981, expresses Congress' intent that federally funded waste treatment and management projects be overall treatment systems and that they constitute the most economical and cost-effective combination of treatment works capable of meeting the Act's requirements.

Legislative Issues

Without enactment of the 1981 Municipal Wastewater Treatment Construction Grant Amendments, Title II issues — both substantive and funding issues — could have been the "forcing mechanism" which would have prompted early Congressional attention to amending the Federal Water Pollution Control Act. With passage of the 1981 amendments, however, it is generally accepted that the next reauthorization of the Act will deal instead with non-Title II issues — that is, issues dealing more directly with industrial dischargers.

While Title II issues are not expected to be considered in depth during the next reauthorization, however—and certainly not in any reauthorization taking place in 1982 — a number of points made by the House Public Works and Transportation Committee's Subcommittee on Oversight and Investigations in its 1980 report may influence later Title II amendments. Some of those points were addressed as part of the 1981 amendments, but others will be revived in future reviews of Title II. According to the Subcommittee report:

> "This massive Federal program has not yet achieved the levels of cleanup that were expected by 1977 nor will it enable a new 1983 deadline for secondary treatment or the original 1983 and 1985 'goals' of 'fishable and swimmable' water and 'zero discharge of pollutants' to be met."[14]

That House Subcommittee report notes that as of September 1980, fewer than 2,300 municipal wastewater treatment projects had been completed. With a total value of about $2.8 billion—indicating that most of the completed projects involve relatively small plants—and with more than half of the U.S.'s 20,000-plus municipal dischargers still not meeting the Act's 1977 treatment requirements, "the lion's share of the Nation's municipal treatment problem has yet to be addressed."[15]

The Subcommittee report notes that the original estimate of $24 billion in "needs" for meeting the Act's municipal cleanup goals has ballooned to an estimated $167 billion (in 1978 dollars). The Subcommittee report points out several reasons for shortcomings in the construction grants program:

- The task of restoring the Nation's waterways has been consistently underestimated, while the ability of the federal government to administer the mammoth public works program effectively has been "grossly overestimated."[16]
- The level of treatment to be achieved by municipal dischargers by the 1977 deadline — secondary treatment — was defined by EPA in a way which precluded use of less expensive technologies.
- Pressured by the law's tight deadlines and by EPA, states rushed to set stringent water quality standards, which meant requiring advanced levels of treatment at high costs.
- Beyond the expanded costs of the program, "delays caused by uncertainties over funding levels, massive red tape, serious understaffing of State and Federal agencies, and the impact of numerous other Federal laws and Executive orders applicable to the program have contributed to the problem."[17] The Subcommittee said that projects which used to take two to three years to complete now are taking eight years, on average, from submission of a planning grant application to EPA through completion of construction.
- Pointing to uncertainties over future funding as "one of the most frequently cited reasons for the slow rate of progress," the Subcommittee urged the Congress to consider the program's long-term needs. "Year-to-year stability of appropriations as well as authorizations is essential to providing proper management and efficient progress."[18]
- With the program characterized from the beginning by excessive paperwork

and complicated regulatory requirements—"red tape unsurpassed in quality and abundance"—the Subcommittee said the program desperately needs a period of stability and predictability, free of all but the most essential program changes. The Subcommittee noted that the excessive paperwork requirements associated with the grants program are the result not only of the law itself but also the EPA's extensive policy guidance documents and implementing regulations.

- Application of new regulations retroactively has been a persistent problem, the Subcommittee said, and should be the exception rather than the rule.
- A persistent shortage of qualified and experienced staff to run the grants program has contributed to delays in achieving the goals set for the program, in the Subcommittee's view.

TITLE III
STANDARDS AND ENFORCEMENT

Title III of the Clean Water Act is unquestionably the most comprehensive portion of the statute. It is also the most controversial, because it applies to industrial sources of water pollution. This section says what levels of pollution control must be achieved by both industrial and municipal dischargers, and it establishes deadlines by which the increasingly more stringent treatment requirements must be attained.

In addition, Title III provides for the establishment of performance standards for new water pollution sources. It deals with effluent limitations for toxic water pollutants and establishes requirements for sources to "pretreat" wastes prior to discharging those wastes to treatment works. It also authorizes public agencies to inspect, monitor and enter discharging facilities in order to enforce the Act's provisions; and provides for pollution-specific programs to address spills of oil and hazardous substances and thermal discharges.

Section-By-Section Analysis
Section 301 (Effluent Limitations)

Section 301 of the Clean Water Act rejects the water-quality standards approach to pollution control. It expresses the zero-discharge concept by saying that "the discharge of any pollutant by any person shall be unlawful" except as those discharges comply with other provisions of the law.

The 1972 Federal Water Pollution Control Act Amendments Section mandated that in order to achieve the objectives of the Act:

- Point sources discharging pollutants into navigable waters (other than publicly-owned treatment works) had to install by July 1, 1977, the "best practicable control technology currently available" (BPT) as defined by the EPA Administrator under Section 304(b).

- Publicly-owned treatment works by July 1, 1977, were to have achieved effluent limitations based on secondary treatment as defined by the EPA Administrator under Section 304(d)(1).

In addition, the 1972 Amendments required that industrial sources comply with a more stringent "best available technology economically achievable" (BAT) by July 1, 1983, and that municipal plants meet "best practicable wastewater treatment technology" by that same 1983 deadline.

Along with meeting BPT and secondary treatment requirements by 1977, industrial and municipal sources under the 1972 Amendments were required to comply with applicable water quality standards where those tighter controls were deemed necessary because of an area's particularly polluted receiving waters.

But in amending the Act in 1977, Congress established three categories of industrial pollutants and created the following controls strategy:

- *Conventional pollutants*
  - — Examples: biological oxygen demand (BOD), total suspended solids (TSS), fecal coliform bacteria, pH (acidity), and other pollutants designated by EPA as conventional.
  - — Treatment required: best conventional technology (BCT).
  - — Deadline: July 1, 1984.
  - — Variances allowed: None.
- *Toxic pollutants*
  - — Examples: an "initial list" of toxics based on the *NRDC* v. *Train* consent decree. The Amendments authorize EPA to add to or subtract from that list.
  - — Treatment required: best available technology (BAT).
  - — Deadline: July 1, 1984, for all toxic pollutants included in the "initial list" of pollutants.* For any additional pollutants added to the list by EPA, the BAT deadline is not later than three years after establishment of effluent limitations.
  - — Variances allowed: None.
- *Nonconventional pollutants*
  - — Examples: those "gray area" pollutants not subject to BAT/toxics regulation or BCT/conventional treatment.
  - — Treatment required: Best available technology (BAT).
  - — Deadline: July 1, 1984, or within three years of promulgation of applicable effluent limitations, whichever is later — but in no case later than July 1, 1987.
  - — Variances allowed: EPA has discretion under the Act to allow treatment levels less stringent than BAT but no less stringent than BPT. These less stringent controls can be permitted if a discharger demonstrates either that the lower level represents the maximum control economically achievable and will lead to "reasonable further progress" toward the 1985 zero-discharge goal, or that the lesser control is environmentally acceptable.

Additional provisions in Section 301 include the following:

- Section 301(d) requires that effluent limitations for meeting the 1984 deadlines be reviewed at least every five years and revised as appropriate.

- Section 301(f) makes it unlawful, notwithstanding other provisions in the law, for sources to discharge "any" radiological, chemical or biological warfare agent or high-level radioactive waste into navigable waters of the United States.

- The 1977 BPT deadline can be extended to July 1, 1983, for industrial dischargers that had contracted with a publicly-owned treatment works to discharge wastes, if the publicly-owned treatment works is not able to accept the discharge.

---

* See Appendix for list of designated pollutants.

- EPA was authorized to extend to April 1, 1979, the 1977 BPT deadline if an industrial discharger had acted in good faith to meet the deadline but had been unable to do so.

- The Act authorizes extensions to July 1, 1987, of the 1984 BAT deadline for nonconventional and toxic discharges to allow replacement of existing pollution-control capacity with an innovative production process. The new process must lead to greater pollution control or lower cost, and must be applicable industry-wide.

Section 302 (Water Quality Related Effluent Limitations)

This section originated in the Senate bill leading to the 1972 Amendments. It authorizes the EPA Administrator to establish effluent limitations more stringent than those authorized under Section 301 upon a determination that the 301 limitations would interfere with attainment or maintenance of acceptable water quality.

Before establishing any more stringent effluent limitations, EPA has to announce its intent to do so and, within 90 days, hold a public hearing to consider the economic and social effects of achieving the more stringent controls. In that decision, the EPA Administrator is to consider economic and social dislocation in the affected community, as well as social and economic benefits resulting from attaining the more stringent effluent limitation. If an affected discharger demonstrates that no reasonable relationship exists between the economic and social costs and the benefits, the EPA Administrator is to modify the effluent limitation as it applies to that particular discharger.

Section 302 was not amended in Congress's 1977 deliberations, and it remains in the law as it was passed in 1972.

Section 303 (Water Quality Standards and Implementation Plans)

Section 303 establishes a procedure by which states adopt (subject to EPA review and approval) what amount to ambient water standards expressing permissible quantities of pollution allowed in designated segments of water bodies. The water quality standards so adopted—including water quality criteria, designated uses for the particular segment, and enforcement mechanisms—are frequently expressed both quantitatively and qualitatively: not more than X micrograms per liter or Y parts per million, or leading to surface waters free of floating debris, scum and other floating materials.

Section 303(d)(1)(A) requires states to identify waters within their boundaries for which Section 301 effluent limitations are "not stringent enough to implement any water quality standard applicable to such waters." Ranking those waters by priority, and considering both existing water pollution and usage (drinking and recreation, growth and propagation of fish and other aquatic and semi-aquatic life), the states are to establish "the total maximum daily load" for pollutants. That load is to be set "at a level necessary to implement the applicable water quality standards with seasonal variations and a margin of safety which takes into account any lack of knowledge concerning the relationship between effluent limitations and water quality."

Both the waters identified and the daily load limits established are to be submitted for EPA approval. The Act requires EPA to set the water quality standards if the state fails to establish approvable standards on its own.

As a condition of having a state water pollution discharge permit program approved by EPA under the Act, Section 303 requires that each state have approved by EPA a continuing planning process. This process must result in plans for controlling water pollution in all navigable waters within a state. At a minimum, those plans are to include:

- effluent limitations and compliance schedules at least as stringent as those mandated in Sections 301, 306 and 307 of the Act and at least as stringent as those contained in applicable water quality standards;
- all elements of applicable Section 208 areawide waste treatment management plans and of applicable Section 209 basin plans;
- total maximum daily load limits for thermal pollutants;
- procedures by which the plan can be revised;
- authority for intergovernmental cooperation;
- adequate implementation and compliance schedules for revised or new water quality standards;
- controls over disposition of residual wastes resulting from water treatment processing;
- an inventory and priority ranking of needs for construction of waste treatment works to meet requirements of Sections 301 and 302.

Section 304 (Information and Guidelines)

This section expresses specific requirements for the EPA Administrator to develop and make public criteria or information, guidelines, factors, procedures and analyses needed to meet the goals or specific requirements of the Act.

It requires the Administrator, for instance, to develop and publish criteria based on the latest scientific knowledge on identifiable health and welfare effects of water pollutants in a water body. The criteria must also cover concentrations and dispersal of pollutants through biological, physical and chemical processes; effects of pollutants on the biological community; and factors affecting rates of eutrophication and rates of organic and inorganic sedimentation for different kinds of receiving waters.

The section provides for EPA development of criteria, information and regulations on effluent limitations consistent with BAT and BPT, and their publication in the *Federal Register.* Guidelines for identifying and evaluating the nature and extent of nonpoint sources of pollutants and processes, procedures and methods for controlling them should be developed. EPA criteria should also cover alternative and innovative wastewater treatment processes; pretreatment of water pollutants determined to be not susceptible to treatment by publicly-owned treatment works; and processes, procedures and operating methods resulting in reduction or elimination of water pollution discharges from new sources.

Section 305 (Water Quality Inventory)

The Senate Committee on Public Works (now known as the Senate Committee on Environment and Public Works), in its report on the Federal Water Pollution Control Act Amendments of 1971 (Report No. 92-414), deplored the "inadequate and incomplete" information on current water quality. The Committee Report continued:

> The fact that a clearly defined relationship between effluent discharge and water quality has not been established is evidence of that information gap. The fact that mixing zones have been permitted is indication of the information gap. The fact that assimilative capacity has been the essential factor in the existing control program is evidence of the information gap. The fact that many industrial pollutants continue to be discharged in ignorance of their effect on the water environment is evidence of the information gap.[18]

To address that problem, Congress in Section 305 directed EPA, with state cooperation, to prepare a report on the "specific quality" of all navigable waters and waters of U.S. contiguous zones. The report is to include an inventory of all point sources of discharge, including a qualitative and quantitative analysis of the discharges. The report (which under the 1977 Amendments should be revised every two years) is to identify specific bodies of water with water quality sufficient to provide for protection and propagation of a balanced shellfish, fish and wildlife population and to allow recreational activities. Also to be identified are those water bodies which will not achieve such water quality until 1977 and 1983, and those reasonably expected to attain that water quality at some later date.

Section 306 (National Standards of Performance)

Section 306 expresses a philosophy common to the regulation of pollution sources: that new sources not be constructed and operated unless they apply the "best" pollution control technology.

The 'new source' strategy reflects a consensus that new sources and substantial modifications of existing sources should install the best available control technology, processes, operating methods or other approaches to reduce pollution. It also recognizes that the reduction of pollution can frequently be achieved more economically in a new facility, in which control equipment can be included in planning and design, than in an existing facility where equipment has to be retrofitted.

Section 306 mandates that the EPA Administrator establish new source performance standards, to be uniform nationally, capable of achieving best available demonstrated control technology. The Act specifies 27 individual categories of industrial sources for which the EPA Administrator is to adopt performance standards, and it authorizes EPA to add others to the list.

Section 306 calls for the performance standards to apply to sources for which construction commences after publication of proposed regulations for that particular industrial category. It authorizes EPA to delegate the new source permitting responsibilities to states which have developed a new source implementation and enforcement program, once the EPA Administrator has approved those programs. In addition, Section 306 gives new sources constructed to meet applicable performance standards a 10-year exemption from having to meet more stringent standards of performance.

Section 307 (Toxic and Pretreatment Effluent Standards)

Section 307 of the Clean Water Act deals with effluent standards for toxic pollutants and for pretreatment of wastes prior to their discharge to publicly-owned treatment works (POTW).

The section dealing with toxic water pollutants is a substantial revision of the 1972 Amendments, Congress having determined that the procedural difficulties in the 1972 legislation had effectively impeded regulatory control of toxics. In the 1977 Amendments, Congress adopted as an "initial list" of toxic water pollutants those specified in a consent decree reached by EPA and the Natural Resources Defense Council over the control of toxic pollutants. Congress said EPA could add to or remove pollutants from that list after considering toxicity of the pollutant, its persistence and degradability, usual or potential presence of affected organisms and the importance of those organisms, and the nature and extent of the effects of the toxic pollutant on the organisms.

The toxic water pollutants are subject to Section 301 and 304 best available technology effluent limitations, to be achieved no later than July 1, 1984. In setting the effluent standard, the EPA Administrator is to provide an "ample margin of safety." The standards are to be effective within one year of promulgation, unless the EPA Administrator determines that deadline to be "technologically infeasible." In that case compliance is required at the earliest feasible date, but at most within three years of adoption of the standard.

In establishing authority for pretreatment effluent standards, Congress was specifically addressing water pollutants which are incompatible with treatment by publicly-owned treatment works. Congress was seeking to regulate pollutants which pass through the treatment works inadequately treated, interfere with operation of the treatment works, or contaminate its sludge byproduct.

Section 307(b) authorizes the EPA Administrator to adopt pretreatment standards to prevent such discharges, with a compliance date within three years of adoption of the pretreatment standards.

To assure that new sources not cause violations of pretreatment effluent standards, the Act directs the EPA Administrator to adopt pretreatment standards simultaneously with Section 306 new source performance standards for equivalent industrial source categories.

Congress amended Section 307 as part of the 1977 Amendments to specify that a treatment works owner or operator can "credit" a discharger if the treatment works removes all or part of any toxic pollutant. If the treatment works' discharge meets effluent limitations, or standards applicable to the toxic pollutant if it were discharged from a source other than a publicly-owned treatment works, the credit also applies. Effluent reductions attained by the treatment works and used to justify a modification of pretreatment requirements must be a permit condition enforceable against the owner or operator.[19]

Section 308 (Inspections, Monitoring, and Entry)

Section 308 requires the owner or operator of any effluent source to install and maintain pollution control equipment, including monitoring equipment and methods. Owners must also provide to the EPA Administrator information based on sampling of the effluent.

The Section authorizes the EPA Administrator or a designate to enter the premises of water pollution sources, and to examine and copy records and reports which must be kept on the water pollution and environmental impacts of the pollution. Those records and reports are to be made available to the public unless they are found to be confidential or to contain trade secrets.

States can develop and submit for EPA approval procedures under state law for inspecting, monitoring and entering water pollution point sources. EPA is authorized to delegate the enforcement responsibilities to the states upon determining that their programs are comparable to the federal program required under Section 308.

Section 309 (Federal Enforcement)

Section 309 of the Clean Water Act requires the EPA Administrator to notify a polluter and the state in which the source is located when the Administrator finds the source in violation of conditions or limitations specified in applicable discharge permits or other permits under the law. If the state has not "commenced appropriate enforcement action" within 30 days, EPA is required to issue a compliance order specifying limitations or conditions the source must meet, or to bring a civil action requiring compliance.

If the EPA Administrator finds violations of permit conditions or limitations to be "so widespread" that it suggests the state is not enforcing the permit conditions satisfactorily, EPA is to notify the state. If "such failure" continues for more than 30 days, the Act directs that EPA make public notice and require the state to satisfy EPA that it will enforce the permit provisions. During the period of "federally assumed enforcement," EPA is to enforce those permit provisions itself.

Sources willfully or negligently violating the Act's provisions are liable for fines of up to $25,000 per day or imprisonment for up to one year, or both. For a second or subsequent conviction, the fine may go as high as $50,000 per day, and imprisonment may be for up to two years, or both. Persons knowingly falsifying reports or documents required under the Act can be fined up to $10,000 or imprisoned for up to six months or both.

In the 1977 Amendments, Congress made some significant changes to Section 309. Concerning the 1977 best practicable technology deadline for industrial sources, Congress authorized issuance of an enforcement order requiring a "reasonable" time for compliance, rather than requiring compliance within 30 days (a deadline widely recognized to be impractical and counterproductive). The 30-day compliance requirement was retained for operation and maintenance requirements and for interim compliance schedules.

The 1977 Amendments also authorize up to 18 additional months for meeting the 1977 deadline if the EPA Administrator finds that the discharger acted in good faith to meet that deadline, and has made a serious commitment to comply by no later than April 1, 1979. EPA must also find that providing an extension will not lead to the imposition of additional controls on other sources; that the source had filed for a permit before December 31, 1974; and that necessary pollution abatement facilities are being constructed.

Congress also authorized extensions to July 1, 1983, for sources discharging to publicly-owned treatment works (if that is the appropriate means of compliance) if failure to comply resulted from reasons beyond their control, "such that it is not appropriate to label them as violators."[20] This amendment sanctioned the enforcement policy which EPA, confronted with the impracticalities of an across-the-board treatment deadline, had already established administratively.

In addition to authorizing BPT extensions for industrial sources which had planned to discharge into a POTW, Congress provided a similar extension for industries which had received innovative technology grants and which, through no fault of their own, had been unable to perfect those technologies. In providing EPA guidance on these extensions, the Senate and House conferees said:

> A person who wishes an extension must have made a serious commitment of the necessary resources to achieve compliance as soon as possible after July 1, 1977, but no later than April 1, 1979. Here the Administrator must determine whether purchase orders were executed, land cleared, and engineers and construction workers available, or other steps taken to insure that the job can be completed by the new extended date.[21]

Another Section 309 Amendment passed in 1977 provides that the EPA Administrator may notify a state and the owner or operator of a treatment works upon finding that any source is discharging to the treatment works in violation of pretreatment standards set under Section 307. Unless the owner or operator of the treatment works takes appropriate action against the source within 30 days, EPA is authorized to initiate a civil action seeking relief. Such relief includes—but is not limited to — seeking a permanent or temporary injunction against the owner or operator of the treatment works. The District Court in which the civil action is brought could restrain the violation and require the owner or operator of the treatment works and of the source to comply with the Act.

Water Quality Standards/Technology-Based Standards

As discussed earlier, Congress in 1972 made the fundamental decision that water pollution control efforts should be based primarily on technology-based effluent standards, with water quality standards reflecting quality of receiving waters relegated to a supporting role. Congress in the 1977 Amendments reaffirmed that judgment.

Although few observers think it likely that Congress will soon revert to a water quality standards-based statute, the fundamental issue of water quality vs. technology-based standards will undoubtedly be a consideration in any overall review of the Act. The issue is likely to be seen not in terms of whether water quality standards should replace technology-based standards, but rather in terms of the extent to which the two basic philosophies can complement each other.

With overall improvements in water quality nationwide, there is increasing concern that nationwide reliance on uniform technology-based standards can lead to "treatment for treatment's sake," without regard for resulting benefits to a particular waterway. This concern results in part from a belief that water quality improvements resulting from imposition of the Act's BPT requirements have been greater than had been anticipated. Some business interests, for instance, point out that existing BPT effluent limitations are reducing discharges of water pollutants to a far greater extent than had been anticipated when major amendments were adopted in 1972. They maintain, therefore, that careful analysis should proceed before more stringent and more expensive technology-based requirements are imposed.

Aware of the somewhat surprising and unexpected results from BPT effluent limitations, Senate and House conferees acting on the 1977 Clean Water Act Amendments said:

> The conferees recognize that best practicable technology has proven more stringent in many instances than anticipated. Consequently, the application of effluent limits based on those regulations will result in a larger measure of progress toward the achievement of the goals of the Act.[23]

That viewpoint is shared by the House Subcommittee on Oversight and Review, which said in its December 1980 report:

> It is now known that basic biological treatment technologies do in fact remove considerable quantities of the toxic priority and other pollutants, and in many instances either reduce or eliminate the threat of both acute and chronic toxicity to the aquatic environment ... [As] to the presence of priority pollutants, testimony to the Subcommittee revealed that far fewer toxic priority pollutants in significantly smaller amounts are often present in treated industrial and municipal effluents than was previously assumed. Even the EPA now forecasts that many industries will be able to achieve the more stringent BAT requirements of the law with their current level of treatment.[24]

Again, there is not likely to be a major effort to convince Congress to return to a water quality standards-based statute. But the unexpectedly good results from BPT technology lead directly to questions about the benefits of more stringent effluent limitations — and that inevitably raises the water quality standards/technology-based standards issue. Adding to the debate is the expectation of still further water quality gains if municipal treatment works—for which compliance with the Act's first-stage control requirements has been far less than for industrial dischargers—attain more stringent controls.

Best Available Technology (BAT)Limitations

Perhaps the most important issue from industry's perspective is the range of questions coming under the BAT limitations umbrella. These issues generally break down in the following way:

- Are the 129 "priority pollutants" adopted in the 1977 Water Act Amendments and based on the *NRDC* v. *Train* consent decree indeed the correct focus for the nation's toxic water pollution control efforts? Should some toxics be added to or eliminated from that list? And if so, based on what criteria?

- Should there be waivers authorized on a case-by-case basis so that some designated toxic discharges would not have to meet BAT effluent limitations? Proponents of such waivers are likely to point to the finding of the House Public Works and Transportation Subcommittee on Oversight and Review that the "priority pollutants" on which the Act has focused since 1977 "are less evident in both amounts and concentrations than previously believed."[25] The subcommittee also recommended that the Act be amended to allow case-by-case modifications of BAT discharge permits if a discharger can demonstrate, based on biological testing, that its effluent poses no threat of acute or chronic toxicity to the aquatic environment.[26]

- What is the proper role of the *NRDC* v. *Train* consent decree in continued implementation of the Act, given that Congress incorporated the thrust of the consent agreement into law as part of the 1977 Amendments?

Section 310 (International Pollution Abatement)

If a duly constituted international agency finds water pollution endangering the health or welfare of persons of a foreign country, and if the U.S. Secretary of State requests action, the EPA Administrator is to notify the state control agency overseeing the source or sources of the cited water pollution.

The Section provides for the convening of a public hearing by the EPA Administrator, establishment of a five-member hearing board, and public announcement of the board's decision concerning the purported international pollution problem. EPA, acting on the board's findings and recommendations, is authorized to take appropriate enforcement actions.

Section 311 (Oil and Hazardous Substance Liability)

Section 311 specifically addresses oil and hazardous substances pollution. It adopts as policy a no-discharge philosophy: "It is the policy of the United States that there should be no discharges of oil or hazardous substances into or upon the navigable waters of the United States, adjoining shorelines, or into or upon the waters of the contiguous zone."[22]

The Section directs the EPA Administrator to adopt regulations designating as hazardous substances those elements and compounds posing imminent and substantial danger to public health or welfare, including fish, shellfish, wildlife, shorelines, and beaches. EPA is to determine also the quantities which would make discharges of each substance harmful. Acting under that authority, EPA has determined that discharges violating water quality standards or causing a visible film, sheen or discoloration of the surface water violate the Section.

The Section prohibits discharges of oil or hazardous substances in quantities determined to be harmful. It requires persons in charge of vessels or of onshore or offshore facilities to report to the U.S. Government such discharges "immediately." Persons failing to provide such notification are subject to a fine of up to $10,000, imprisonment for not more than one year, or both. Owners or operators of violating sources are subject to fines of up to $5,000 for each offense.

Section 311 authorizes the President to act to remove or arrange for removal of spilled oil or hazardous substances. It directs the preparation, publication and revision of a National Contingency Plan for removal of oil and hazardous substances. The plan will assign duties and responsibilities among federal departments and agencies, in coordination with state and local agencies, as well as identification, procurement, maintenance and storage of clean-up equipment. A trained task force will be designated to carry out the plan, including establishment of trained emergency task forces at major ports. The plan will also include a system of surveillance and notice, so that appropriate federal agencies will be immediately notified of discharges and of imminent threats of discharges; and procedures and techniques to be used in identifying, containing, dispersing and removing oil and hazardous substances.

With certain exceptions (act of God, act of war, negligence on part of U.S. Government), owners or operators of violating sources are liable to the U.S. Government for clean-up costs. For inland oil barges, the financial liability to a violator is limited to $125 per gross ton or $125,000 whichever is greater. For other vessels, the liability ceiling is $150 per gross ton or, for a vessel carrying oil or hazardous substances as cargo, $250,000, whichever is greater. Congress adopted those liability ceilings as part of the 1977 Amendments in recognition that the previous $14,000 ceiling had made it very difficult for water carriers to obtain adequate insurance coverage. If the United States can show that the discharge resulted from "willful negligence or willful misconduct within the privity and knowledge of the owner," the owner or operator is liable for the full amount of the clean-up costs.

For owners or operators of onshore violating facilities, the liability ceiling is $50 million; but again the ceiling is eliminated if the U.S. shows willful negligence or misconduct. For both onshore and offshore facilities, Congress authorized the President to specify that the maximum liability limit not exceed $50 million and that the minimum limit be not less than $8 million.

Section 312 (Marine Sanitation Devices)

Section 312 regulates water pollution discharges from marine sanitation devices. It authorizes EPA, after consultation with the Coast Guard, to adopt federal performance standards designed to prevent discharges of untreated or inadequately treated sewage. The Section does not apply to vessels *not* equipped with toilet facilities.

The section "grandfathers" existing vessels with sanitation devices, and it specifies that the initial performance standards were to be applicable two years after they were adopted.

For commercial vessels operated on the Great Lakes, Congress mandated that the EPA marine sanitation device standards require, at a minimum, the equivalent of secondary treatment as defined under Section 304(d).

Section 312 forbids manufacturers of marine sanitation devices to sell, offer for sale, introduce or deliver into interstate commerce, or import into the U.S. for sale or resale devices not approved under the law.

Section 313 (Federal Facilities Pollution Control)

Section 313 requires federal agencies and facilities to comply with all provisions of the Act, including payment of reasonable service charges and fees, to the same extent as nongovernmental entities. The President may exempt a source if he thinks it is "in the paramount interest" of the United States to do so; however, no exemptions are available from new source performance standards, or from toxic pollutant or pretreatment effluent standards.

Section 314 (Clean Lakes)

This section calls for states to submit to EPA a report on the eutrophic conditions of publicly-owned freshwater lakes, ways of controlling pollution in those lakes, and ways of working with federal agencies to restore the lakes' water quality.

It also provides federal funding for use in preparing the clean lakes analyses.

Section 315 (National Study Commission)

Section 315 established the National Commission on Water Quality—consisting of five Senators, five members of the House of Representatives and five members appointed by the President—to study aspects of meeting or not meeting the 1983 fishable/swimmable goals of the Act. The Commission was authorized funding of up to $17.25 million, and it submitted its final report and recommendations to the Congress in 1976.

Section 316 (Thermal Discharges)

Section 316 authorizes the EPA Administrator to revise limitations on the thermal component of a discharge if the source demonstrates that the applicable effluent limitation would be more stringent than needed to assure protection and propagation of a balanced indigenous population of shellfish, fish and wildlife.

The Section requires that standards adopted under Sections 301 and 306 specify that the location, design, construction and capacity of cooling-water intakes reflect best technology available for minimizing adverse environmental impacts.

Section 317 (Financing Study)

Section 317 directs the EPA Administrator to analyze alternate financing methods for preventing, controlling and abating water pollution. It authorizes appropriations of up to $1 million for conduct of the study.

Section 318 (Aquaculture)

After public hearings, the EPA Administrator can permit discharges of specific pollutants under controlled conditions associated with an approved aquaculture project so long as the source is permitted under Section 402.

Section 318 directs EPA to adopt regulations specifying appropriate procedures and guidelines. It also says states wanting to administer their own programs can do so after EPA determines that their programs are adequate to meet objectives of the Act.

Legislative Issues

As the most comprehensive and most substantive portion of the Clean Water Act, Title III—Standards and Enforcement is likely to figure prominently in any overall review and reauthorization of the Act.

The Title III issues in large part involve answers to the following questions: How much water pollution control has been achieved and will be achieved as a result of compliance with the Act's "first stage" best practicable technology requirements? How much additional control can be expected from imposition of the more stringent best available technology requirements, and what will be the cost?

To what extent are the nonconventional or nontraditional pollutants, including toxic water pollutants, treated as a result of BPT requirements? If more stringent controls are necessary and warranted, what deadlines are practical for requiring sources to attain the more stringent controls?

This section of the report discusses specific Title III issues which Congress probably will be asked to consider in reauthorizing the Act.

Some business interests undoubtedly will maintain that the court action was superseded by the 1977 amendments. They will argue that the consent decree should be abandoned, in part because it unduly hampers and constrains EPA actions in carrying out parts of its responsibilities under the Act by specifying criteria and actions not required by the law. Environmental groups, on the other hand, will point out that the consent decree "goes further" than Congress did and that its features are essential to effective control of toxic water pollutants. They will point out too that the agreement represents "good faith" negotiations between them and the Executive Branch and should be honored to the extent possible.

Some observers believe that the debate over the consent decree is more emotional and symbolic than substantive. They point out too that the issue raises interesting philosophical and constitutional questions concerning *who* writes laws — Congress or the courts?

Best Available Technology (BAT) Deadline

The Clean Water Act Amendments of 1977 require industrial dischargers to achieve by July 1, 1984, a level of treatment known as best available technology for the 129 priority pollutants specifically listed by Congress on the basis of the *NRDC* v. *Train* consent decree. (This agreement is often called the "Flannery Decision" after U.S. District Court Judge Thomas A. Flannery of the District of Columbia, under whose jurisdiction the agreement was negotiated.) Under that agreement BAT effluent limitations were to be established for each priority pollutant and included in discharge permits of some 14,000 dischargers classified in 21 specific industrial categories.

The agreement also called on EPA to develop water quality criteria for each of the priority pollutants. It gave the agency 42 months to complete the work, so that industry could have appropriate control equipment in place and operating in time to meet the July 1, 1983, deadline (which Congress extended by one year in 1977).

Pointing to inadequate funds, time, data and analytical methodologies, EPA has subsequently acknowledged that the deadlines it had agreed to under the consent decree had been impractical. "It is clear," EPA Administrator Douglas M. Costle said in a letter to the principal plaintiff, NRDC, "that the task has proven to be far more resource-intensive and time-consuming than originally perceived."

NRDC and EPA, under Judge Flannery's jurisdiction, agreed in 1979 to amend the original consent decree and adopt a new schedule for setting the BAT effluent limitations. They agreed to focus not on 21 industrial categories but rather on 34 categories. They also extended the December 1979 court-approved deadline for issuing final effluent standards to March 1981. But as many predicted at the time, and as EPA itself appeared to acknowledge, the new deadlines also have not been met as planned. As a result, there are likely to be numerous calls for the compliance deadline to be extended again.

The House Subcommittee has acknowledged the problems facing EPA in attempting to regulate toxic water pollutants in a timely and effective way:

> Current efforts to move the toxics control program off dead center are still beset by such an array of problems as to call into grave question whether the EPA is truly capable of putting into effect a genuinely workable, legally defensible and cost-effective regulatory scheme with which industry and local government can reasonably be expected to comply within the statutory deadline.[27]

Because the agency has been unable to provide BAT regulations in time to provide for "orderly and efficient" controls, the Subcommittee said, Congress should specify a BAT deadline of no later than July 1, 1987, for pollutants other than toxics. For toxics, the Subcommittee said the Act should be amended to allow for case-by-case modification of BAT permits if a discharger can demonstrate, based on biological testing, that its effluent will not threaten acute or chronic toxicity to the aquatic environment.

The notion of case-by-case extensions is one which might be acceptable also within the environmental community. Attorneys for NRDC have recognized that "a certain amount of lead time is necessary following promulgation in order to write permits as well as finance, construct and test the treatment facilities."[28]

Saying that extensions should be considered on a case-by-case basis and not across-the-board—"A delay across-the-board could provide more time than necessary for some industries and not enough for others"—three NRDC attorneys have pointed to "the psychological and enforcement benefits" of firm deadlines. "We would favor a provision for case-by-case extensions based on a demonstration of need, a showing of good faith, and other criteria," they said. "But the associated burdens on enforcement and permitting personnel must be weighed carefully."[29]

Pretreatment

Certain to be among the most controversial issues considered as part of a Clean Water Act reauthorization is the pretreatment program. This program is intended to address industrial facilities which discharge not directly into the nation's waters but rather into a publicly-owned treatment works, which for a fee treats the industrial wastes prior to discharging directly to a water body.

Indicative of the controversy is this statement from the House Subcommittee:

> Of all the toxics-control provisions of the Act aired at the [Subcommittee] hearings, EPA's handling of pretreatment was subjected to the most compelling criticism. Witnesses from states, metropolitan sewerage agencies and industry variously condemned the evolving pretreatment requirements as unworkable, as well as needlessly complex, confusing and certain to lead to costs totally out of proportion to any environmental benefits derived. Treatment for treatment's sake was the common complaint.[30]

The issues likely to be most controversial as part of a Congressional debate on the pretreatment program, each of which is discussed in further detail below, are the following:

- *Local control:* Is the current dependence on national technology-based standards appropriate? Can such a strategy adequately consider the exent to which a discharge interferes with operation of a treatment works, or the extent to which a municipal treatment works adequately removes pollution? What is the most effective division between federal and state/local responsibilities?

- *Removal credits:* In an effort to avoid "redundancy" — unnecessary duplication of treatment — Congress in 1977 established a mechanism so that local treatment plant officials, subject to EPA guidance and approval, could "credit" an industrial discharger for the amount of a restricted pollutant already being removed by a publicly-owned treatment plant. Critics complain that EPA's implementation of the removal credit provisions makes the program unworkable, leading to unnecessarily expensive treatment without providing sufficient water quality benefits.

- *Sludge disposal:* Congress in the 1977 Amendments expressed its interest in disallowing removal credits if they would result in high concentrations in a municipal treatment works' sludge (the residue left over from wastewater treatment). To keep the vast quantities of municipal sludge relatively free of toxic contaminants, so that it can be disposed of beneficially through processes such as land spreading, the pretreatment program is intended in part to concentrate chemical wastes in industrial rather than municipal sludges.

- *Costs/benefits:* With pretreatment, as with so many environmental control programs, the issue of relative costs and benefits is likely to be controversial. Critics say costs of a pretreatment program—and certainly of a program *not* carried out in the most efficient and effective manner—far outweigh benefits to water quality or the environment generally.

- **Local control**

In response to Section 307(b) of the Act, EPA has developed a pretreatment program based on national, technology-based pretreatment standards applicable to industrial facilities discharging toxic and nonconventional pollutants. Industry critics say this approach does not adequately take into account the extent to which a discharge in fact interferes with operation of a POTW and the extent to which the discharge is satisfactorily treated by the treatment works. Pointing to wide variations in the mix of wastes to be treated at individual municipal plants, critics say the unique problems facing a POTW are best considered at the local level and not through national standards. If an industrial facility's discharge causes or contributes to a violation of a treatment works' discharge permit (see discussion in next chapter under Section 402), the municipal officials should develop and enforce pretreatment limits for that source, they say.

The House Oversight and Review Subcommittee has recommended elimination of national pretreatment standards, saying that EPA, eight years after enactment of the 1972 amendments, had been "almost totally unsuccessful" in carrying out the pretreatment program. Recommending implementation of industrial pretreatment programs "without further delay," the Subcommittee said the Act should be amended so that local treatment plant authorities can establish pretreatment requirements on the basis of their discharge permits.[31] EPA and states should adjust their existing permit programs to strengthen POTW discharge permit requirements designed to control toxic pollutants, the Subcommittee said. "In order to assist the states and municipalities in this effort, EPA should take the necessary steps to provide them with a better understanding of the amounts of toxic chemical removal which can be achieved by *all* forms of treatment currently being used by local wastewater treatment authorities."

In the environmental community, discussions of increasing local responsibilities for pretreatment raise concerns over the possibility of "no-strings-attached" local responsibility. Representatives of environmental organizations characterize the pretreatment program as seeking to control toxic effluents unless it is demonstrated (through the removal credits provision discussed below) that the treatment is unnecessary. They say critics of pretreatment would reverse the burden of proof, making control of toxics unnecessary unless it was proved to be required.

Citing estimates that more than one-half of toxic pollutant loadings entering POTWs come from industrial sources, attorneys for NRDC have said:

> The current pretreatment program attempts to place at least a major portion of this cleanup burden on those industries, with the expectation that associated costs will be reflected in higher product prices and therefore generate incentives for source [pollution] reduction. The alternative of relying on municipal treatment means that up to 75 percent of those costs could be borne by the taxpayer, and no direct incentives are generated. There are no workable mechanisms by which industrial sources are required to pay for the portion of municipal treatment costs needed to handle their wastes.[32]

Without adequate mechanisms for assuring that industrial facilities pay their share of treatment costs, environmental representatives say, the general public must foot the bill—a bill totalling billions of dollars annually.

The financial arguments are not the only concerns environmental community representatives express about shifting the pretreatment program into local hands. They point out that many municipal treatment works still have not installed required biological control treatments mandated by the Act, and they say it will be many years and many billions of dollars—at least—before POTWs will accomplish the toxic pollution reductions now being estimated.

Relying on municipal treatment works' discharge permits to trigger the need for industrial pretreatment programs is also rejected by the environmental community. It would take many years to establish scientifically-defensible toxic effluent limits for the POTWs, they say, and once established an enormous monitoring program would be required so that municipal authorities could decide if pretreatment is necessary. How will a municipal plant know if its permit violations result from discharges from industrial, residential or nonpoint pollution sources? they ask.

• *Removal credits*

Congress, wanting to insure that the 129 "priority pollutants" specified in the *NRDC v. Train* consent decree would be treated to limits meeting best available technology requirements, also sought to avoid redundant treatment.

In theory, the pretreatment by the industrial facility *plus* the consistent treatment of the wastewater by the treatment works should equal BAT. To avoid redundant or excessive treatment — and thus unnecessary costs — industrial facilities were to be "credited" with the treatment carried out by POTWs.

In practice, critics contend, it hasn't worked out that way. They say that regulatory obstacles established by EPA make the granting of removal credits extraordinarily complex and difficult. Without those credits, industry has to install expensive control technology to meet pretreatment requirements even though the POTW may in fact remove all or most of various pollutants in the discharger's effluent. The result is redundant treatment, say critics.

On this point, the House Subcommittee has said that the "complex requirements, ambiguities in technical definitions, and numerous costly and detailed administrative requirements for calculating removal credits" have prompted many municipal officials to decide that the credit provision is either impractical or unworkable.[32]

Environmentalists agree, at least to a point. Saying there are "legitimate reasons" that the removal credits provisions are "complex and demanding," NRDC attorneys nonetheless agree that modification of those provisions is "essential."[33] The NRDC representatives say they too are concerned that EPA's implementing regulations are so difficult to carry out that some municipalities simply will not use the provision.

A reliable yet simple means of calculating credits must be found, but doing so will be difficult, they say. "Congress should at least consider a series of *national* credits that are calculated by EPA through detailed studies of various types and sizes of municipal systems. These credits would be less precise, but could be applied to a pretreater without great burdens on municipalities."[34]

To avoid the situation of vesting more responsibilities in local authorities already widely recognized to have inadequate resources, the NRDC attorneys offer three suggestions:

- Allow more time for the control of water pollution from sources discharging to POTWs or so-called indirect dischargers.

- Institute a "greatly simplified program."

- In lieu of the credits program, depend instead on gross assumptions about municipal systems' removal capabilities.

According to the three NRDC attorneys:

These suggestions should be taken seriously. There is no denying that this program is complex, perhaps too complex, for municipalities to implement with existing resources and within existing deadlines. The program should be simplified somewhat, and, we believe, more resources must be authorized if the pretreatment effort is to succeed. But the answer to these problems is not to abandon pretreatment standards. A carefully drafted middle ground must be found that maintains the philosophical basis for the program while streamlining and clarifying it. We see the need for a much larger role for the states, a simplified credit, and perhaps some adjustments to the deadlines.[35]

• *Sludge*

Wastewater treatment produces large volumes of waste residuals referred to as sludge, and that sludge itself must be disposed of in an environmentally acceptable way. As the House Subcommittee puts it: "Overshadowing the administrative and technical complexities of pretreatment itself, there is a major continuing problem of what to do with the sludge left over from pretreatment. Many toxic chemicals are not destroyed in the treatment process and end up in the sludge. This is, of course, a problem for industry and municipalities alike."

Concerned with the potential for large quantities of municipal sludge so contaminated with toxic wastes that it would be useless for landfill and other benign disposal, Congress in 1977 adopted a provision restricting the granting of removal credits if they would lead to high toxic concentrations in municipal sludge. To address the sludge contamination issue, environmentalists want to see firm deadlines established for EPA to adopt sludge disposal guidelines under the Act (see Section 405 discussion in next chapter). Only with these guidelines can the removal credit provision be reasonably and knowledgeably carried out, they say.

• *Costs/Benefits*

The perennial costs/benefits considerations in most environmental programs are also an issue in the pretreatment program, according to the House Subcommittee. Pretreatment critics testified that costs and benefits of carrying out EPA national uniform standards "are significantly out of balance," the Subcommittee says. "Many of those testifying argued strongly that a pretreatment system based on water quality standards and a municipal treatment plant's discharge permit requirements would better ensure that excessive levels of control, redundant treatment and needless costs could be avoided."[36]

The costs/benefits issue will raise the difficult question of whether incremental pollution reductions are worth the proportionally higher costs they frequently involve, both in terms of limited resources and benefits to receiving waters.

Additional Title III Issues

While BAT limitations, BAT deadlines and pretreatment are the three sets of Title III issues likely to be most prominent in any comprehensive review of the Clean Water Act, several other Title III issues also warrant attention.

• *Water Quality Criteria and Standards*

Some industry critics have expressed concern that EPA is improperly imposing its own Section 304(a)(1) water quality criteria on states in their adoption of water quality standards under Section 303 of the Act. They say the law does not authorize EPA to require states to use those criteria in adopting state standards.

These critics object that EPA thinks of fishable/swimmable use designations as the norm in developing state water quality standards. They say EPA allows less stringent designations in only a few circumstances. That approach should be abandoned, industry critics maintain, and states should be able to set water quality standards based on multiple water uses.

As the Chemical Manufacturers Association says in an October 1981 Clean Water Act position paper:

We believe that EPA's information criteria under Section 304 should not be presumptively applicable. Section 303 should provide for multiple use designations and the adoption of standards designed to ensure that such uses are maintained. Fishable/swimmable waters, though a laudable goal, should not be the rule in all cases, particularly when background pollutants in the water would make achievement of fishable/swimmable quality impossible.[37]

In addition, CMA and other critics of the current Act are likely to recommend improved peer review processes to better ensure the technical integrity of water quality criteria published by EPA.

• *Best Conventional Technology (BCT) Limitations*

Some industry critics of the Act are concerned that EPA has not adequately applied cost-effectiveness criteria in determining whether pollution control more stringent than best practicable technology (BPT) is required for conventional pollutants. In deciding that the more stringent best available technology (BAT) need not be applied to specified conventional pollutants, Congress in the 1977 Amendments established the best conventional technology (BCT) limitation. Section 304(b)(4) said that EPA, in determining BCT, must consider the reasonableness of the relationship between costs of reducing the effluent and the resulting benefits. Also to be considered is "a comparison of the costs and level of reduction of such pollutants from the discharge from publicly-owned treatment works to the cost and level of reduction of such pollutants from a class or category of industrial sources."[38]

Critics of EPA's handling of its responsibilities under this section of the Act feel the agency should base its decisions on a comparison with average costs of secondary treatment rather than on a comparison with incremental costs of advanced treatment. They say EPA's reliance on the advanced treatment comparison results in an inaccurate and complex methodology, and in more stringent treatment for conventional pollutants than intended by Congress.

• *New Source Standards*

Some critics of the Act say separate technology-based new source performance standards are unnecessary because EPA, in practice, has adopted standards identical to BAT limitations for industrial sources. This, they say, places an increased administrative burden on the agency without providing water quality benefits.

TITLE IV
PERMITS AND LICENSES

Title IV of the Clean Water Act provides for the issuance of discharge permits to point sources discharging pollutants into navigable waters of the United States. It provides also for the issuance of permits for dredged or fill materials. It requires applicants for federal permits or licenses to certify that their discharge complies with effluent limitations and water quality-limited limitations under Sections 301 and 302 of the Act.

In addition, Title IV provides for establishment of criteria for disposal of wastes into the oceans, territorial seas, or contiguous zone of the U.S. It also calls for regulation of the disposal of sewage sludges.

Section-By-Section Analysis

Section 401 (Certification)

Applicants for federal water pollution permits or licenses under Section 401 of the Water Act must provide a certification from the state in which the pollution originates or will originate. The state certification must show that the discharge complies with applicable provisions of Sections 301, 302, 303, 306 and 307 of the Act.

Section 401 provides that the state or interstate agency (or in certain cases the EPA Administrator) must act on the request for certification within one year of receiving it or the certification requirement is effectively waived. Federal licenses or permits to conduct activities leading to discharges to navigable waters are not to be issued unless and until the certification is granted.

The section establishes a procedure by which another state can challenge issuance of a certification if it believes the resulting discharges will affect its water quality. It provides for public hearings and the conditioning of a license or permit as necessary to assure protection of water quality. Federal licenses or permits issued pursuant to a certification can be suspended or revoked by the federal agency if the certified facility or activity is found to be operating in violation of applicable provisions of Section 301, 302, 303, 306, and 307 of the Act.

Section 402 (National Pollutant Discharge Elimination System)

Section 402, in many respects the backbone of the entire Clean Water Act, establishes a procedure by which point sources discharging pollutants to navigable waters receive permits authorizing the discharges. Point source discharges of pollutants to navigable waters of the U.S. are unlawful without applicable permits issued either by the federal government or by states delegated the permits program.

In establishing the National Pollutant Discharge Elimination System (NPDES) in Section 402, Congress specified that the discharge permits be conditioned to assure that discharges meet applicable requirements of Sections 301, 302, 306, 307,

308, and 403 of the Act. The conditions established by the permitting agency can involve not only quantity, quality and flow rate of the discharge but also data and information requirements and reporting requirements.

In establishing the NPDES program, Congress intended that it be administered primarily by state agencies and not by the federal government. In Section 402(b), Congress established a mechanism by which a state's governor and legal official can adopt a state program comparable to the federal permitting program and seek delegation of the program from EPA (the federal agency initially charged with carrying out the permits program).

Congress specified criteria which must be met by a state in order for it to be delegated the permits program:

- The state program must have adequate authority to issue permits applying Section 301, 302, 306, 307, and 403 requirements and ensuring compliance with them.
- The state permits must be for periods of no more than five years, after which time the permits must be re-issued and, if necessary, revised.
- The permits must be conditioned so that they can be terminated or modified "for cause"—for instance, violations; misrepresentation or incomplete disclosure of all relevant facts; or changed conditions requiring temporary or permanent reduction or elimination of the permitted discharge.
- The state must have authority to control disposal of pollutants into wells.

The NPDES program can be delegated to a state only if the state demonstrates that it has adequate enforcement authorities, including inspection, monitoring and source entry authority. The state must adopt public notification and public hearing procedures and provide EPA a notification and copy of each permit application. It must also assure that industrial sources discharging to publicly-owned treatment works comply with Sections 204(b) (user charges provision to see that users pay for their "proportional share" of POTW operation), 307 (toxic and pretreatment effluent standards) and 308 (inspection, monitoring and entry provisions).

The Act authorizes the EPA Administrator to withdraw a state's NPDES delegation after a public hearing if the EPA Administrator finds the program is not being carried out in accordance with the Act. In actual practice, however, no state NPDES program has ever been withdrawn, and it is highly unlikely that many—or perhaps any—will be.

The NPDES program applies not only to industrial facilities discharging pollutants from a point source to navigable waters, but also to municipal treatment works.

Section 403 (Ocean Discharge Criteria)

Section 403 sets standards applying to permits for discharges into the territorial sea, contiguous zone or ocean. It says that Section 402 NPDES permits cannot be issued unless they comply with ocean discharge criteria established by EPA under Section 403.

Congress in Section 403 directed that EPA adopt and revise as necessary guidelines for determining degradation of territorial sea, ocean, and contiguous zone waters. The criteria are to include:

- effects of disposal of pollutants on human health or welfare and on sealife and beaches;
- effects on marine life, including diversity, productivity and stability of the marine ecosystem and changes in marine species and community population;
- effects of the pollutant disposal on esthetic, recreation and economic values;
- persistence and permanence of pollutant disposal effects;
- effects of disposal at varying rates of pollutant volumes and concentrations;
- other possible locations and means of disposal or recycling, including land-based disposal alternatives; and
- effects on alternate uses of oceans, such as mineral exploration and scientific study.

Where "insufficient information" exists on a proposed discharge to allow a "reasonable judgment" on its compliance with any of the established guidelines, no discharge permit is to be issued, Congress said in Section 403(c)(2).

Section 404 (Permits for Dredged or Fill Material)

The Section 404 dredged or fill material program is administered by the Army Corps of Engineers through guidelines established by EPA. It provides for the issuance of permits regulating discharges of dredged of fill materials (such as result from excavation or deepening of river channels) into navigable waters at specified sites.

The guidelines established by EPA after consultation with the Secretary of the Army are to be based on criteria comparable to those specified under the Section 403 ocean discharge program described above. Discharges receiving Section 404 discharge permits are exempted from the Section 402 NPDES permits program.

The scope of the 404 program depends largely on the definitions of dredged or fill materials to be regulated under it and of "navigable waters" to which the program applies. The other parameters are the remedies available to permitting agencies in controlling discharges, and the criteria for selecting disposal sites and issuing permits.[39]

The 404 program generally applies to material excavated or dredged from navigable waters. Congress in the 1977 Amendments specified that the program generally *not* apply to the following categories:

- material from normal farming, silviculture and ranching activities;
- material discharged for the purpose of maintaining or repairing recently damaged parts of structures such as dikes, dams, levees, breakwaters, causeways, bridge abutments or approaches and transportation structures;
- material discharged in order to construct or maintain farm or stock ponds or irrigation ditches;
- material discharged for the purpose of constructing temporary sedimentation basins on a construction site;
- discharges of materials for building or maintaining farm roads, forest roads or

temporary roads for moving mining equipment, so long as "best management practices" are applied to minimize adverse impacts; and

- discharges resulting from activities subject to an approved state Section 208 areawide management plan and meeting requirements of Section 208.

In Section 404 Congress specified a mechanism by which states could assume the dredged or fill material permitting responsibilities after demonstrating that they have "adequate authority" to carry out the program. Section 404(h)(1)(A) specifies conditions which state programs must meet in order for the state to be delegated the program. Like the Section 402 NPDES program, the 404 permitting program can be withdrawn from an approved state upon the EPA Administrator's finding, after a public hearing, that a state is not carrying out the program as specified in the Act.

Section 404(s) authorizes enforcement of the dredged or fill materials program. It authorizes the Army Secretary to issue orders requiring persons violating a permit condition to comply, and the Secretary is authorized to initiate a civil action to enforce the program.

Persons willfully or negligently violating any permit condition or limitation are liable for penalties of between $2,500 and $25,000 per day of violation or imprisonment of up to one year, or both. For second and subsequent convictions, an offender can be fined up to $50,000 per day of violation and imprisoned for up to two years, or both. Persons violating a permit condition or limitation are subject to a civil penalty of up to $10,000 per day of violation.

Section 405 (Disposal of Sewage Sludge)

In Section 405, Congress mandated that disposal of sewage sludge resulting from operation of a publicly-owned treatment works is subject to Section 402 NPDES permitting requirements if any pollutants in the sludge would enter navigable waters.

Congress directed EPA to adopt regulations governing issuance of permits for disposal of sewage sludge. Those regulations are to apply the same criteria, factors, procedures and requirements that apply to a Section 402 permit, as the EPA Administrator sees fit in order to carry out objectives of the Act. Like other permitting programs under the Act, the sludge disposal permitting program also can be delegated to states, so long as the state shows it can carry out the program in accordance with Section 402.

Congress expanded Section 405 as part of the 1977 Amendments. It directed the EPA Administrator, after consultation with interested federal and state agencies and other interested persons, to publish guidelines for disposal and use of sludge. Those guidelines, in addition to identifying uses and disposal, are to specify factors to be considered in determining means of each use or disposal. They also must identify concentrations of pollutants interfering with each use or disposal.

Legislative Issues

Heading the areas of likely legislative interest under Title IV of the Clean Water Act are the two major permitting programs—the Section 402 NPDES program and the Section 404 dredged or fill materials program. The 402 program affects more individual sources and is more widespread geographically. It is therefore likely to generate more general interest, although the 404 program in past years has proven to be at least equally contentious.

Section 402 (NPDES Permits Program)

The House Subcommittee on Oversight and Review, after holding hearings in 1980 on the NPDES program, concluded that it agreed with state water pollution control officials who had criticized the program. The Subcommittee found that the program is "on the verge of collapse, at least in terms of its ability to be used to put into effect national uniform standards for industry clean-up." [40]

The Subcommittee summarized its views of the NPDES program as follows: [T]he NPDES permit program is the primary regulatory mechanism for accomplishing the law's objectives. This is the mechanism for applying the BAT, pretreatment and other requirements of the law to individual dischargers. It is no stranger to controversy, being plagued by problems since its inception. It was seen ideally as a straightforward approach to ensuring that all of the Nation's dischargers would know just what they were to accomplish, when it had to be done, and what the penalties for failure would be. A piece of paper, a permit issued by U.S. EPA or by the state, theoretically was to tell it all, succinctly and clearly. Unfortunately, the permit program has become a paper-shuffling game of monumental proportions. [41]

Characterizing the program as a "paper chase," the Subcommittee pointed out that the issuance of permits to individual sources was to be dependent on establishment of specific Title III effluent limitations for separate industry categories. EPA, however, has been unable to issue most of the industrial effluent limitations in time for permitting officials to use them, in part because of lack of data and in part because of industry court challenges to EPA regulations. Many EPA regulations were overturned by courts which found them based on poor information and therefore technically indefensible.

Lacking final regulations on which to base permit decisions, federal and state permit writers instead had to issue nearly 60,000 industrial permits based on "best professional judgment:" a combination of limited knowledge of water quality and engineering common sense. In only a few instances was the potential presence of toxics considered, the Subcommittee continued. That case-by-case approach did little to guarantee the national uniformity Congress had intended.

Another problem identified by the Subcommittee is that the self-monitoring system crucial to the NPDES program appears to have left open the potential for widespread and frequent noncompliance with permit conditions and limitations. The Subcommittee pointed to research suggesting that most dischargers had major deficiencies in one or more of the general areas of flow monitoring sampling techniques and analytical techniques.

The House Subcommittee pointed to several factors contributing to a troubled institutional relationship among the federal and state agencies involved in carrying out the NPDES program. First, it pointed to a "Washington-knows-best" attitude on the part of EPA, which has led to excessive second-guessing of state permitting decisions. In addition, state and local agencies are "overwhelmed" by detailed federal regulations. Third, EPA resists suggestions that state and local agencies become real partners in the permits process, the Subcommittee said.

The legislative solution to many of these problems is fairly clear, in the Subcommittee's opinion. Rather than having NPDES permits issued for a period of five years as under the current law, the Subcommittee thinks permits should be issued for eight or ten years. The longer permit period would give the NPDES program more stability and certainty and would make better use of limited EPA and state regulatory staffs, the Subcommittee indicated.[42]

The longer permit duration is an idea likely to be favored also by other critics of the current NPDES program. Among other NPDES reform proposals likely to be advanced:

- Limit to rare and specified cases the opportunity for EPA to revise permit conditions or limitations during the duration of the permit, in order to avoid the discharger's having to chase a "moving target;"
- Require EPA to set technology-based effluent limitations on permits only on adopted effluent limitation guidelines, avoiding case-by-case decisionmaking and reserving "best professional judgment" BAT permit limits for significant toxic problems; and
- Restrict EPA's authority to veto state-issued NPDES permits.

Section 404 (Dredged or Fill Materials)

Along with the 402 permits program, the Section 404 dredged or fill materials permitting program is likely to prompt calls for amendments in the next reauthorization of the Clean Water Act. While the 404 program directly affects fewer industrial dischargers and is somewhat more restricted geographically, historically 404 amendments have generated substantial controversy.

Critics of Section 404 implementation are likely to argue that the program has become increasingly bogged down with redundant environmental impact reviews, unnecessary costs and long delays in permitting. There are concerns that the Corps of Engineers, in carrying out the 404 program, at times has gone beyond its traditional role in regulating impacts on navigation and navigable capacity of the Nation's waterways. Some critics feel that the Corps is seeking to regulate environmental impacts best left to EPA or state pollution control agencies.

In addition, Congress could be asked to amend the Water Act so that the "navigable waters" for which 404 permits are required are defined more narrowly. This would reverse a federal court ruling, *NRDC* v. *Callaway*, holding that the Corps had to revise implementing regulations to reflect the expanded definition of navigable waters resulting from enactment of the 1972 Federal Water Pollution Control Act Amendments. Such legislation would require fewer dredged or fill activities to be subject to 404 permits.

Another issue which Congress may face is whether to have EPA rather than the Corps of Engineers handle the 404 program. Some critics of the current program are likely to suggest that EPA be authorized to issue 404 permits.

TITLE V
GENERAL PROVISIONS

Title V of the Clean Water Act involves general administrative, judicial review and procedural provisions, and it is not expected to involve major controversy in a reauthorization of the Act. As is clear to all persons with experience in environmental programs, however, the "procedural" and "substantive" sections of an act are not always clearly defined, and the importance of certain aspects of Title V cannot be overlooked.

Section-By-Section Analysis

Section 501 (Administration)

This section authorizes the EPA Administrator to adopt regulations necessary for carrying out functions mandated to EPA. It gives the Administrator and the Comptroller General of the United States or their authorized representatives access to books, records and documents of grant recipients so they can audit the grants. Grant recipients must undertake recordkeeping as prescribed by the EPA Administrator, so that disposition of the grant and total project costs can be evaluated.

Section 502 (General Definitions)

This section provides Congress' word-by-word definitions of terms as they are used in the Clean Water Act. Section 502 specifically defines 19 terms used in the Act— terms such as "pollutant," "navigable waters," "effluent limitation," "discharge of a pollutant," "toxic pollutant," "point source," "biological monitoring," "schedule of compliance," "industrial user," and "pollution."

Section 503 (Water Pollution Control Advisory Board)

This section establishes within EPA an advisory board consisting of the EPA Administrator or designee and nine members appointed by the President from among persons not employed by the federal government. The section specifies administrative details for the board, which is to advise, consult with and make recommendations to the EPA Administrator on EPA responsibilities under the Act.

Section 504 (Emergency Powers)

This section authorizes the EPA Administrator to bring suit on behalf of the United States to immediately restrain pollution deemed to present an "imminent and substantial endangerment" to health or welfare. Congress made clear in this section that it considered endangerment to livelihood sufficient to warrant EPA court action; it used as an example of welfare impact the inability to market shellfish.

In the 1977 Amendments Congress added language to Section 504 saying EPA can provide assistance in emergencies resulting from discharges, and it established a contingency fund of up to $10 million for providing that assistance. The new language directs the EPA Administrator to report annually to Congress on activities taken in carrying out the emergency powers provision. It also said EPA could provide such emergency assistance whenever the Administrator determines:

- the assistance is immediately required to prevent, limit, or mitigate an emergency;
- there is an "immediate significant risk" to public health or welfare and the environment;
- the assistance will not otherwise be provided in a timely way.

Section 504 language adopted in 1977 says that costs of assistance provided for emergencies resulting from violations of Section 301, 306, 307, 402, or 403 provisions are recoverable from the owner or operator of the violating source. The funds are to be recovered through Section 309 federal enforcement provisions.

Section 505 (Citizen Suits)

This section authorizes any citizen of the United States to commence a civil action against water pollution sources or against the EPA Administrator, the latter only in the event of failure to perform a nondiscretionary duty.

The section requires plaintiffs to give 60 days notice of an alleged violation, and it disallows citizen actions if the EPA Administrator or a state is prosecuting a civil or criminal action to require compliance. In these cases the citizen is only allowed to intervene in the case. For violations of new source standards under Section 306 and toxic effluent standards under 307(a), Section 505 waives the 60-day advance notification requirement.

For purposes of bringing citizen suits under Section 505, the term "citizen" is defined as any person or persons having an interest which is or may be adversely affected by the discharge of a pollutant.

Section 506 (Appearance)

This section authorizes the EPA Administrator to request that the Attorney General of the United States represent the Nation in a civil or criminal action brought under the Act and involving EPA. The Attorney General must notify EPA "within a reasonable time" that he will appear in a civil action, or else attorneys with EPA can represent the government in the case. The Act does not authorize EPA attorneys to represent the government in criminal actions.

Section 507 (Employee Protection)

This section is designed to protect employees from harassment, discharge or discrimination as a result of their filing or causing to be filed an enforcement proceeding against their employer for a Clean Water Act violation. It protects employees so that they may testify in enforcement proceedings.

Employees who feel they were discriminated against in violation of Section 507 have 30 days in which to apply to the Secretary of Labor for a review of the firing or other discrimination. The Labor Secretary, after hearings and an investigation as he deems appropriate, can order remedies including reinstatement with compensation.

Section 507(e) requires the EPA Administrator to conduct continuing evaluations of losses or shifts in employment resulting from issuance of any effluent limitation on order under the Act.

Section 508 (Federal Procurement)

This section "blacklists" persons convicted of violations under Section 309(c) — federal agencies cannot contract with those persons or source owners or operators for goods, materials or services if the contract is to be performed at any facility where the violation giving rise to the conviction occurred. The prohibition on federal procurement lasts until the EPA Administrator certifies that the violating condition has been corrected.

Section 508 directs that the President require all federal agencies to carry out the procurement prohibition. It also authorizes the President to exempt certain contracts, loans or grants from the procurement prohibition if an exemption is in the "paramount interest" of the United States.

Section 509 (Administrative Procedure and Judicial Review)

This section authorizes the EPA Administrator to issue subpoenas to gain the attendance or testimony of witnesses and to obtain relevant papers, books and documents in carrying out information-gathering functions under Section 305 water quality inventory responsibilities.

Section 510 (State Authority)

Section 510 allows states, their political subdivisions or interstate agencies to adopt and enforce standards more stringent than the federal standards if they want to. It makes clear that the states may not impose less stringent standards, but it leaves them free to apply more stringent standards.

Section 511 (Other Affected Authority)

This section makes it clear that the Clean Water Act does not limit authorities or functions of other American agencies under other laws or regulations not inconsistent with the Water Act. It makes clear too that the Act does not alter the Corps of Engineers' responsibilities under the 1899 Refuse Act to maintain navigation, except that Section 404 permits are substituted for the Section 10 permits required under the Refuse Act.

Section 512 (Separability)

This section makes clear that if one part of the Clean Water Act is held invalid as it applies to any person or circumstance, application to others is not affected.

Section 513 (Labor Standards)

This section specifies that laborers and mechanics employed by federally-funded publicly-owned treatment works are paid wages not less than those prevailing for the same work in the immediate vicinity, as specified under the Davis-Bacon Act.

Section 514 (Public Health Agency Coordination)

This section directs Section 402 permitting agencies (federal EPA or a designated state agency) to assist permit applicants in coordinating Clean Water Act requirements with requirements of appropriate public health agencies.

Section 515 (Effluent Standards and Water Quality Information Advisory Committee)

Section 515 establishes within EPA a nine-member advisory committee appointed by the EPA Administrator. It specifies that committee members have adequate training and background to provide, assess and evaluate scientific and technical information on effluent standards and limitations. Members shall serve for four years and then be eligible for re-appointment.

Section 516 (Reports to Congress)

Section 516 specifies that the EPA Administrator must report to the Congress annually on a range of water pollution control issues.

It directs that the EPA Administrator, in cooperation with states, make a detailed estimate of costs of carrying out the Act. Every other year EPA and the states must estimate construction costs for needed publicly-owned treatment works.

In the 1977 Amendments, Congress directed EPA to submit by October 1, 1978, a report on the status of combined sewer overflows in municipal treatment works. Congress said that report could include recommendations for legislation to address those overflows. Also by that date, EPA was to provide for Congress a report on the status of use of municipal secondary effluent and sludge for agricultural and other uses.

Section 517 (General Authorization)

Section 517 authorizes maximum appropriations for carrying out the Clean Water Act. The enabling committees of Congress authorize the maximum appropriations, and then the appropriations committees make available funds up to the maximum appropriations.

Section 518 (Short Title)

This section, the last section of the Clean Water Act, says the Act may be cited as the Federal Water Pollution Control Act, commonly referred to as the Clean Water Act.

Legislative Issues

Title V of the Clean Water Act is unlikely to be a major focus of amendments during a reauthorization of the statute, but several legislative initiatives nonetheless can be expected.

For instance, there could be calls for Congress to require that EPA rulemaking be subject to economic impact analyses and perhaps cost-benefit analyses, in an effort to assure that regulations are cost-effective. In addition, some parties have expressed interest in requiring EPA to consider not only the economic impact of a particular regulation on an affected interest but also the cumulative impact on an industry or company of other regulatory programs, so that the total economic impact of federal regulations on a facility can be calculated.

Other possible amendments affecting administration of the Water Act could involve procedures by which regulatory agencies gain access to corporate information and means by which trade secrets and proprietary information are protected from unlawful disclosure. Some parties have expressed concern that inadequate handling of corporate information could impair voluntary exchanges of information between industry and the regulating community.

Another administrative procedure common at EPA also may attract criticism during the reauthorization process. The agency has often issued policy guidance documents to regional offices and state and local water pollution control agencies regarding implementation of certain aspects of the Act. Those guidance documents are not subject to the public comment and open hearings provisions applicable to more formal rulemaking, and critics have complained that they nonetheless have the force of regulation in terms of meeting requirements of the Act. To correct the situation, critics may ask that Congress specify that guidelines, manuals, guidance documents, instructions, criteria, and other policy documents be subject to public notification and availability requirements and judicial scrutiny, just as regulations are.

APPENDIX

The following is the initial list of designated pollutants under *NRDC* v. *Train*.

Acenaphthene
Acrolein
Acrylonitrile
Aldrin/Dieldrin
Antimony and compounds*
Arsenic and compounds
Asbestos
Benzene
Benzidine
Beryllium and compounds
Cadmium and compounds
Carbon tetrachloride
Chlordane (technical mixture and metabolites)
Chlorinated benzenes (other than dichlorobenzenes)
Chlorinated ethanes (including 1,2-dichloroethane, 1,1,1-trichloroethane, and hexachloroethane)
Chloroalkyl ethers (chloromethyl, chloroethyl, and mixed ethers)
Chlorinated naphthalene
Chlorinated phenols (other than those listed elsewhere; includes trichlorophenols and chlorinated cresols)
Chloroform
2-chlorophenol
Chromium and compounds
Copper and compounds
Cyanides
DDT and metabolites
Dichlorobenzenes (1,2-, 1,3-, and 1,4-dichlorobenzenes)
Dichlorobenzidine
Dichloroethylenes (1,1- and 1,2-dichloroethylene)
2,4-dichlorophenol
Dichloropropane and dichloropropene
2,4-dimethylphenol
Dinitrotoluene
Diphenylhydrazine
Endosulfan and metabolites
Endrin and metabolites
Ethylbenzene
Fluoranthene

49

Haloethers (other than those listed elsewhere; includes chlorophenylphenyl ethers, bromophenylphenyl ether, bis(dichloroisopropyl) ether, bis(chloroethoxy) methane and polychlorinated diphenyl ethers)

Halomethanes (other than those listed elsewhere; includes methylene chloride, methylchloride, methylbromide, bromoform, dichlorobromomethane, trichlorofluoromethane, and dichlorodifluoromethane)

Heptachlor and metabolites

Hexachlorobutadiene

Hexachlorocyclohexane (all isomers)

Hexachlorocyclopentadiene

Isophorone

Lead and compounds

Mercury and compounds

Naphthalene

Nickel and compounds

Nitrobenzene

Nitrophenols (including 2,4-dinitrophenol and dinitrocresol)

Nitrosamines

Pentachlorophenol

Phenol

Phthalate esters

Polychlorinated biphenyls (PCBs)

Polynuclear aromatic hydrocarbons (including benzanthracenes, benzopyrenes, benzofluoranthene, chrysenes, dibenzanthracenes, and indenopyrenes)

Selenium and compounds

Silver and compounds

2,3,7,8-tetrachlorodibenzo-p-dioxin (TCDD)

Tetrachloroethylene

Thallium and compounds

Toluene

Toxaphene

Trichloroethylene

Vinyl chloride

Zinc and compounds

---

*As used in this Appendix, the term 'compounds' includes organic and inorganic compounds.

LIST OF REFERENCES

Magazine Articles

Barton, Kathy; "The Other Water Pollution." *Environment,* Vol. 20, June 1978; pp. 12-20.

Hall, Ridgway M., Jr.; "The Clean Water Act of 1977." *Natural Resources Lawyer,* Vol. 11 No. 2, 1978; pp. 343-372.

Keith, Larry L. and William A. Telliard; "Priority Pollutants." *Environmental Science and Technology,* Vol. 13, April 1979; pp. 426-433.

Ward, Morris A.; "Amending the Clean Water Act." *The Environmental Forum,* Vol. 1, No. 4, August 1982; p. 5.

Westman, Walter E.; "Problems in Implementing U.S. Water Quality Goals." *American Scientist,* Vol. 65, March-April 1977; pp. 197-203.

Government Reports

U.S. Environmental Protection Agency, Office of Water Program Operations: "1980 Needs Survey: Cost Estimates for Construction of Publicly-Owned Wastewater Treatment Facilities." Washington, 1981. 93 p. (PRD-29)

U.S. General Accounting Office, Report to the Congress by the Comptroller General of the United States:
"An Executive Summary: 16 Air and Water Pollution Issues Facing the Nation." Washington, 1978. 43 p. (CED-78-148A; October 11, 1978)

"Many Water Quality Standard Violations May Not Be Significant Enough to Justify Costly Preventive Actions." Washington, 1980. 78 p. (CED-80-86; July 2, 1980)

U.S. General Accounting Office, Report to the Administrator, Environmental Protection Agency:
"A New Approach Is Needed for the Federal Industrial Wastewater Pretreatment Program." Washington, 1982. 18 p. (CED-82-37; February 19, 1982)

"EPA Should Help Small Communities Cope with Federal Pollution Control Requirements." Washington, 1980. 65 p. (CED-80-92; May 30, 1980)

"User Charge Revenues for Wastewater Treatment Plants — Insufficient to Cover Operation and Maintenance." Washington, 1981. 35 p. (CED-82-1; December 2, 1981)

"Water Quality Management Planning Is Not Comprehensive and May Not be Effective For Many Years." Washington, 1978. (CED-78-167; December 11, 1978)

NOTES TO TEXT

[1] Public Law 80-845, Section 2(d)(7).

[2] Public Law 89-234, Section 5(a).

[3] 30 Stat. 1151, 33 U.S.C.A., Section 407.

[4] William H. Rodgers, Jr., *Environmental Law* (West Publishing Company: St. Paul, 1977), p. 359.

[5] *Ibid.*

[6] "Implementation of the Federal Water Pollution Control Act," Report by the House Subcommittee on Oversight and Review, Committee on Public Works and Transportation, (96-71), December 1980, p. 1.

[7] Clean Water Act (Public Law 92-500 as amended), Section 101(a).

[8] Analysis of H.R. 11896, "A Legislative History of the Federal Water Pollution Control Act Amendments of 1972," Committee Print, Volume 1, January 1973, p. 762.

[9] Committee Report No. 92-911, "Federal Water Pollution Control Act Amendments of 1972, H.R. 11896," March 11, 1972, p. 91.

[10] "Joint Explanatory Statement of the Committee of Conference," (95-830), December 6, 1977, p. 68.

[11] *Ibid.*

[12] *Natural Resources Defense Council (NRDC)* v. *Train,* 396 F. Supp. 1386, 1389-90; 5 ELR 20405, 20406; 7 ERC 2066.

[13] "Joint Explanatory Statement of the Committee of Conference," p. 95.

[14] House Subcommittee Report, (96-71), December 1980, p. 3.

[15] *Ibid.*

[16] *Ibid.*

[17] Position Statement, Association of State and Interstate Water Pollution Control Administrators, May 1981, p. 5.

[18] "Federal Water Pollution Control Act of 1971," Report of the Committee on Public Works, U.S. Senate, (92-414), October 28, 1971, p. 55.

[19] Conference Report on H.R. 3199, (95-830), December 6, 1977, pp. 87-88.

[20] *Loc. cit.,* p. 89.

[21] *Ibid.*

[22] Clean Water Act, Section 311(b)(i).

[23] Conference Report, p. 85.

[24] House Subcommittee Report, (96-71), p. 58.

[25] *Loc. cit.,* pp. 29, 30.

[26] *Loc. cit.,* p. 62.

[27] *Loc. cit.,* p. 29.

[28] J. Taylor Banks, Frances Dubrowski, and Jacqueline M. Warren, "Water Quality: What Should be Done *Today?:* A Discussion of Important Issues Facing Policy Makers and Environmental Advocates in the Next Two Years" (Natural Resources Defense Council, Inc.: Washington, D.C., February 12, 1981), p. 36.

[29] *Ibid.*

[30] House Subcommittee Report, (96-71), p. 41.

[31] *Loc. cit.*, p. 62.

[32] "Water Quality: What Should be Done *Today?*", p. 38.

[33] *Loc. cit.*, p. 40.

[34] *Ibid.*

[35] *Loc. cit.*, p. 42.

[36] House Sobcommittee Report (96-71), p. 42.

[37] "Policy Paper on the Clean Water Act" (Chemical Manufacturers Association: Washington, D.C., October 1, 1981), p. 25.

[38] Clean Water Act, Section 304(b)(4).

[39] Rodgers, *loc. cit.*, p. 399.

[40] House Subcommittee Report, (96-71), p. 60.

[41] *Loc. cit.*, p. 52.